Made in Scotland

Made in Scotland

BILLY CONNOLLY

My Grand Adventures In A Wee Country

with

Ian Gittins

3 5 7 9 10 8 6 4

Published in 2018 by BBC Books, an imprint of Ebury Publishing,

20 Vauxhall Bridge Road,
London SW1V 2SA

BBC Books is part of the Penguin Random House group of companies
whose addresses can be found at global.penguinrandomhouse.com

Penguin
Random House
UK

This book is published to accompany the television series entitled *Made in Scotland* first
broadcast on BBC in 2018. *Made in Scotland* is a 7 Wonder production. Directed by
Mike Reilly, Managing Director: Blake Chaplin.

First published by BBC Books in 2018

www.penguin.co.uk

A CIP catalogue record for this book is available from the British Library

ISBN 978 1 785 94370 6
Paperback ISBN 978 1 785 94373 7

Typeset in 11.75/20 pt Bembo Std by Jouve (UK), Milton Keynes
Printed and bound in Great Britain by Clays Ltd, Elcograf S.p.A.

CONTENTS

CONTENTS

· · · · · · · · ·

'I DIDNAE COME FROM NOTHING'

Where do you come from?

It's one of the most basic human questions of all. Luckily, it is easily answered – what kind of prick doesn't know where they were born? But there is another question, which might sound a wee bit similar but is actually very different:

What do you come from?

And, let me tell you, that question can take you all sorts of strange places . . .

Last year, just in case you didn't know, I was knighted. On 31 October 2017, I went down to Buckingham Palace and Prince William put his sword on both of my shoulders and made me Sir William Connolly CBE. I got it for 'services to entertainment and charity'. When I was young, I would have hated the very idea of being given a knighthood. The hippy Billy Connolly would have thought it was all nonsense. But I've mellowed as I've got older and I have come to appreciate being given things by people. If somebody or other in authority wants to tell me, 'You're very good, therefore you're entitled to *this*,' it is a charitable act. They are doing it for the very best reasons and to turn it down would be churlish, in my opinion. *Just take it.* Be nice and appreciate it.

So, I took it and I said, 'Thank you.' It's not like having a knighthood has made any great difference to my life. I don't spend my days now hanging out with other goodly knights or rescuing damsels in distress. The only thing that it has changed is some people's attitudes towards me. I have noticed that some people get a great delight from calling me 'Sir Billy': 'Sir Billy, will you do this, please?' Well, good luck to them, but it doesn't really mean anything to me.

In any case, if I am honest, I didn't really cover myself in glory when I got knighted. Prince William asked me a few questions but I was very nervous, and what with that and my Parkinson's disease, my mouth suddenly stopped working at the most inopportune moment. I flubbered and I bejabbered. The prince asked me something, fuck knows what it was, and I said, *'Flabgerbelbarbeghghghgh.'* Honestly, he must think I am a complete simpleton. I'd love to meet him again to apologise, and to show him that I'm not a total idiot.

After my knighthood was announced, a woman from the BBC came to Glasgow to interview me. We sat down in a lovely hotel in a nice part of town, and she hit me with her first question:

'This must mean a lot to you, with you coming from nothing?'

I looked at her, and I laughed.

'I didnae come from nothing,' I told her. 'I come from something.'

I mean, I have never hidden that I come from humble stock. I grew up in the tenements of post-war Glasgow. In fact, I used to specify exactly where, onstage: it was on a kitchen floor, 'on the linoleum, three floors up'. The early years of my life were spent in grinding poverty ... but it wasn't *nothing*. It was something – something very important. There is this viewpoint that if you have come from the working class you have come from nothing, whereas the middle and upper classes are something, and I don't hold with that opinion. I think the working class is something. It is *everything*. They are the builders of society, and without them the whole house falls down.

I am very proud to be working class, and especially a working-class Glaswegian who has worked in the shipyards. It is something, and don't you forget it. *I come from something.* I come from the work-ing class. And, most of all, I come from Scotland.

It's weird how I always get so closely linked with Scotland. I am probably more famous for being a Glaswegian than for anything I have actually done. Yet I don't mind this focus – in fact, I enjoy it – and I understand it. I have always sounded very Scottish. Nobody is ever going to mistake where I come from. And when I started out, my humour was totally bound up in Scotland and Scottishness. How could it not be? It was what I knew. It was *all* that I knew.

I love Scotland, with a fierce passion that has never dimmed. I love talking about Scotland and, most of all, I love being there. I have lived in America for many years now, but I have never stopped feeling Scottish. Nearly twenty years ago, in a book that she wrote about me, my wife, Pamela, said, 'Billy is constantly drawn back to Scotland. It's as though he'd fade into depression without a regular fix.' Well, it's as true now as it was then. I need to feed from Scotland – from the land, and from the fierce craic of the people.

It's a strange thing to be proud of where you come from. It doesn't really make any sense. After all, it's not something that you have earned or worked for – it's a simple accident of birth. But being Scottish is a very lovely thing. Scotland is a unique and wonderful place. Its national motto says a lot about it: *Nemo me impune lacessit*. 'You will not strike me with impunity.' A decent translation might be: 'By all means punch me in the nose but prepare yourself for a kick in the arse.' J. P. Donleavy explained it well: 'I'll thank you not to fuck about with me.' It's also notable that the national animal of Scotland is a unicorn. Occasionally, people say to me, 'But that's a mythical animal!' To which I answer, 'Oh, yeah? You'll be telling me the Loch Ness Monster is mythical next!' And *that* is Scotland in a nutshell.

Glasgow made me, but I love all of Scotland. There's a beauty and an intensity there it is hard to find anywhere else in the world. The west coast of Scotland, and the Highlands and islands, are probably still my favourite places on the planet. My long-time manager, Steve Brown, who sadly died in 2017, was a farmer for years and he used to tell me how he got great spiritual strength from the soil. He used to sink his arms into it, right up to the elbows, and draw comfort from it. I guess that's how I feel about Scotland. It's a very lovable place.

I would love Scotland just as much even if I didn't come from there. Luckily, I'm steeped in the country and in its culture, which I have absorbed over so many decades. I mean, I'm seventy-five years old now. *Seventy-fucking-five! Me!* I am well versed in Scottish history – although the only problem with reading history is that it tends to be littered with royal families, which I find boring. Royal families always strike me as being like the Mafia, using their family name to conquer people and steal their stuff. Not that I mentioned any of that to Prince William. He might have found another use for that sword. I took the safe option and just said, '*Flahgerbelbarbeghghghgh.*'

The funny thing is that I wasn't offended when the woman from the BBC asked me that daft question. She asked me very nicely, with no malice at all, and it is true that I have always talked about my roots in poverty. I suppose I can see exactly where she was coming from. But she was dead wrong.

I didnae come from nothing: I come from Scotland. And this book is about why I will always be happy and proud that I do.

'DID THE WINDOW BREAK ON BOTH SIDES WHEN YOU THREW THE STONE?'

P. G. Wodehouse, one of my all-time favourite writers and one of the funniest men who ever lived, said, 'It is never difficult to distinguish between a Scotsman with a grievance and a ray of sunshine.' He appeared to feel that my people possess a certain dourness of nature – and he certainly had a point. In fact, the instinctive response of most Scots, confronted with a gorgeous sunny day, is to shake their heads and mutter, 'Ah, we'll pay for this!'

Where does this pessimism come from? I think it is partly from the malign influence wielded over the country for too many generations by religion (and we'll come to that later) – and partly from the bloody weather. There's a great Scottish word that sums up that mix of cold, cloud and drizzle that dominates our climate: *dreich*.

This dreich can draw a pall over the country and drive people into a deep gloom. I don't get that. I've always told my audiences, 'Stop calling rain "bad weather"! Because if rain is bad weather, we're fucked!' Or — 'There is no such thing as bad weather, just the wrong clothes!'

Scots are sometimes perversely proud of being looked on as dour but I don't subscribe to that mindset at all. I have always been a glass-half-full sort of guy. It's just the way I am. I'm an anthropological rarity — a Glaswegian who is a natural optimist. It's probably just as well that I'm like that, because if I wasn't, I could have quite a misery memoir in me.

I've always hated misery memoirs and that shite 'woe-is-me' style of writing. I just don't see the use of it. I also loathe that thing of 'I'm from a working-class slum, didn't I do well?' That whole stance leaves me cold. I meet people like that all the time, who say, 'We came from nothing, haven't we done great?' They always seem to expect me to join in, but I never do. It's all way too smug for my liking. What do they want, a medal? I feel like saying, 'Get over yourself, you prick!' Even so, there is no denying that my early years, whichever way you look at them, were pretty grim.

I was a war baby, born on 24 November 1942, and that made sense, because everyday life pretty soon began feeling like a battlefield. My dad, William, was away with the RAF in Burma so I began life with my mum, Mamie, and my eighteen-month-old sister, Florence, at 65 Dover Street in Anderston, central Glasgow. We lived on the third floor of a tenement block in a tiny two-room apartment. My mum slept in one room and Florence and I slept behind a curtain in a little alcove in the kitchen. We had no bathroom and so we all washed or bathed in the kitchen sink, normally in cold water – hot was virtually unheard of. My cot was a drawer from a sideboard.

It sounds fucking Dickensian but the big point is that we were not the only people living like that. It was the same for everybody around us. People weren't up in arms about their living conditions. We all just accepted it as normal. We might have been surviving, rather than living, in utter poverty but it didn't feel that way to me. When you're a child, what you know is all you know, and I have fond, faded memories of my mum looking after us as I played at home with Florence.

Florence and I would play out in the street every day if we could. Our games were not complex. We'd throw marbles against the kerb or just chase each other around. There was no traffic to worry about. The doctors and the school teachers had cars in 1940s Glasgow, but nobody else did. Dover Street had no shops. It was just all tenements, except for a dark, forbidding church on one side of the street. It didn't seem to have any windows. I guess that those particular devout people worshipped in the dark.

When you see photos of Glasgow from that post-war era they are all in black and white, and I think my memories are as well. Everything is monochrome and sepia. There again, that didn't stop us having some pretty colourful experiences.

A family called Cumberland lived in Dover Street. They were a big family: they had nine children and we'd sometimes play with them. One evening the dad came home from work in the docks – because all the local men worked in the docks – had his tea and told his wife he was off down the pub. His wife was a wee bit pissed off by this announcement and told him in no uncertain terms that he could get their kids in from the street and into bed before he went. Mr Cumberland was desperate for a beer so he went out, grabbed the first nine kids he found and slung them into the bed. Two of the kids he stuffed into bed were Flo and me. Mum couldn't find us and only tracked us down when she found two little Cumberland kids still playing out late, which gave her a wee clue where we might be.

I can still remember lying in that huge bed, amazed at what was happening. Flo whispered to me not to worry, we'd be OK, and I thought the whole thing was hilarious, a joyous adventure. I've told the story on stage for many years, but one night I met one of the grown-up Cumberland kids, who was angry at me for doing so. They said that it made their dad sound like a pisshead. Well, fancy that!

Another time, I was out drawing on the street with a piece of chalk and a policeman caught me. He asked where I lived and was marching me upstairs when Mrs McGee, who lived in the bottom flat below us, came out. She gave him a tongue-lashing – 'Leave the boy alone and go catch some thieves!' – and sent him packing.

There again, the police were a funny lot when I was a kid. After the war there was a lot of immigration into Glasgow from the Highlands because there was no work up there. The women were great nurses and the men became policemen. The Highlands men were huge, round-faced yokels who all seemed to be called Morrison. When I was older, we called them *teuchters*. There'd be jokes about them in the music halls: 'The teuchter asked the boy: "Did the window break on both sides when you threw the stone?"' Or: 'A teuchter found a drunk man asleep on Sauchiehall Street and dragged him into Hope Street because he couldn't spell Sauchiehall Street.'

Like any child, I thought my mum would be there for ever. She was kind and loving and when I was tiny she looked after Flo and me. We never gave a thought to what her life was like – but if I imagine it now, it must have been unbearable. Mum was only seventeen when she had Florence and nineteen when she had me. She was a teenager, looking after two toddlers in a war. The Nazis were dropping bombs on the docks on the Clyde by where we lived. My dad was far away with the RAF: who knew when, or if, he was coming back?

When I was four, Mum met a man who said he loved her. It must have been the first time in years anybody had shown kindness and love to her. He asked her to go away with him and she just got up and left one day, telling nobody, leaving me and Florence behind.

It's strange but, seventy years on, I don't blame my mum for going. It was all too much for her. In any case, even if I did, what would be the point of going through life holding it against her? That kind of anger and resentment eats you up from the inside. It doesn't pay off, in my view.

I still remember the day she went, though, and wasn't there any more, and I was alone in the house with Florence. It wasn't that scary – it was just weird. We got hungry and neighbours heard us crying and called our Auntie Mona, who came around and took us away. Mona took me and Florence to live with her, her sister Margaret and their brother James in their tenement, three or four miles up the road in Stewartville Street in Partick.

It looked, from the outside, as if she was our saviour but, really, Mona was a totally destructive influence on my young life. She mocked me, she beat me and she bullied me. I've no idea, even today, why she would treat her young nephew so badly – was she angry because looking after me and Florence reduced her own chances of meeting somebody, settling down and having a family? Whatever the reason, she made my life, and Flo's to a degree, a misery. Many, many years later, I said this about Mona on TV, on *The South Bank Show*: 'It was very big of her to take on the responsibility [of looking after us] but, having said that, I wish people wouldn't do that. I wish people wouldn't be very big for five minutes and rotten for twenty years. I would rather have gone to a children's home and been with a lot of other kids being treated the same.'

I was about five when my dad came back from the war and moved into the tenement with us. He would take me and Florence out at weekends but the war had damaged him and he never talked about my mum or where she was. He was silent and distant, and he didn't seem to notice how badly Mona treated me. Or, if he did, he didn't do anything about it. Occasionally he'd give me a beating himself if I'd been particularly bad. Pamela was horrified when I first told her that my dad would hit me so hard that I would fly over the sofa backwards, in a sitting position, just like real flying except that I didn't get a cup of tea or a safety belt. But that was what he did every now and then.

Life didn't get any better when I went to school. In fact, it got a whole lot worse. I enjoyed kindergarten and could write by the time I left – but St Peter's School for Boys was something else entirely.

Like a lot of Catholic schools in the 1950s, it had a huge bleeding Christ on a crucifix in the foyer, and that pretty much set the tone of the fucking place. The headmistress, Sister Philomena, had paintings of Hell on her walls. They were probably illustrations from Dante's *Inferno*, but back then I assumed that they were her summer holiday photos.

The teachers put the fear of God into us, literally, psychologically and physically. It's fair to say that the Scottish education system in the Forties and Fifties was not a haven of liberal or progressive thinking and St Peter's was a fearful, violent place. You'd get beaten for any kind of misbehaviour. For talking, messing about, anything. This was bad news for me, as I was always talking and messing about, so I got a lot of nasty leatherings.

The teachers' main weapon was the tawse. This was a leather belt, about a yard long and a quarter-inch thick, with two or three tails, and a rounded point at the other end. Sometimes they'd thrash us with the tails and sometimes with the handle end. Just to mix things up a bit, you know.

We got the tawse from age five or six onwards. The teacher would make you hold out your hands and hit you with it. On a cold and frosty morning, it was really painful. You would be going home with huge welts up your wrists. It seems crazy today to think of adults being allowed to beat children with a piece of leather. And you couldn't ask your parents for any help. If a boy told his dad about it, he would hit him as well, for getting into trouble at school.

I had a teacher called Rosie McDonald who was a complete fucking old psychopath. She belted the shit out of me for years. Her trick was laying pencils on her desk, making you put your hand on them, then beating you with the tawse, to make sure it hurt you even more. Rosie terrorised her class and seemed to pick on me the most. I'd get in to school, aged six, and hang around outside her classroom door, too scared to go in. When another teacher went past and shoved me in the door, she would tawse me for being late. She would thrash me for breaking a pencil, for scruffy homework or for looking out of a window. I did a lot of the last one – I became an expert in the sex lives of pigeons on the roof opposite my class – and so I got belted pretty much every day.

Rosie left an indelible mark on me. Decades later, my daughter, Cara, graduated from Glasgow University and I went to her ceremony. There was a garden party afterwards and as I was stuffing my face with strawberry tart, a guy came up to me.

'Billy, I've never met you before,' he said, 'but I believe you were taught by an auntie of mine.'

'Oh, really?' I said. 'Who was that?'

'Rosie McDonald.'

The second he said it, all my anger came flooding back. I don't think it had ever gone away.

'She was a fucking psychopath!' I said.

'Well, she had her own way of doing things . . .' the guy began.

'No, no, she was a fucking psychopath!' I told him. 'Don't get me wrong!' I was so het up I think I was probably spitting straw-berry tart all over the poor sod.

I just couldn't get on with school. It was a foreign country to me. The lessons made no sense. I used to loathe algebra, and parsing – where you would try to break sentences down into pro-nouns, adverbs, etc. What the hell was the point of that? Nothing in school caught my imagination except for reading. I liked it when the teachers would read us Robert Louis Stevenson, or we'd read it ourselves. But there was nothing else that I liked and I was no good at anything else.

Looking back now, I think I was so fucked up in the head from the atmosphere at home that I couldn't cope with the lessons. Going from Mona's viciousness to Rosie McDonald was a curse that you shouldn't wish on anyone. I think it was bound to end in tears.

My report card used to say, 'Billy has a fertile imagination', and the teachers clearly did not regard this as a desirable state of affairs. My feud with Rosie went on and came to a spectacular head when I stopped doing my homework. I just decided one day not to be part of the stupid school goings-on any longer. Rosie asked me if I had done my homework and I calmly told her that, no, I hadn't.

'What?! Come up here now, Connolly!'

She gave me a good belting with the tawse and did the same thing every single day thereafter when I gave the same answer, but I didn't care. I had had enough. I couldn't be bothered with the system and I opted out.

Sometimes I would hear boys at school telling each other, 'God, I wish my mother would stop kissing me when I'm going to school! I hate it!' As well as having no mum by now, I had also never been kissed since I could remember. I never said anything, but I used to think, '*I* wouldn't mind a kiss from time to time.'

So, it was a pretty wretched time all round, but – fuck it! I already said that I hate misery memoirs, so I'm not about to write one now. It was a horribly bleak time in my life, but I survived it, and there is no doubt in the long run it made me stronger.

I suppose my way of coping was to become the class clown. It was a role that I took to pretty well. I remember one day, when I was about seven, tripping over and falling in a puddle at school, and a whole load of kids gathering round to laugh at me as I sat there. It wasn't that unpleasant in the puddle and I was enjoying the jollity and making everyone happy so much that I carried on sitting there. 'Ah, now *this* is pretty good!' I remember thinking to myself. 'I'll have a bit of this!' I carried this new love of trying to make everyone laugh from the playground into the classroom.

My quick tongue earned me plenty of beatings from Rosie, of course, but so what? You can only take so much pain, physical or otherwise, before you become numb.

And I was having some fun as well. After school, our games in the street included rounders, kick-the-can and cricket with a wicket chalked on a wall, which made it a wee bit hard to knock the bails off. Or we'd just kick a tyre around. One time we found a bus tyre and I squeezed myself into it at the top of a steep hill. The idea was that my pals would push me and I would roll down the hill, across the main road and through the window of a furniture shop. I rolled at great speed all the way down the hill and across the road, but after two blocks the tyre careened off to the left and into a dairy. I came to a sudden halt in a pile of milk crates.

Another great adventure of my young life was flying down the same hill on a sledge, in the snow, and going right under a coal horse as it went about its rounds. That one made me a bit of a local legend, and quite right, too. The milkman and coalman still delivered with horses back then. They used to fly along, sometimes faster than traffic does nowadays. People used to go out in the street with shovels as the horses passed, hoping for manure for their gardens or window boxes. The ragman used to shout, 'Delft for rags!' and Delft was china plates. You'd hang them on your wall, like plaques. We had one of Anne Hathaway's cottage.

Post-war Glasgow was littered with wasteland, bombsites and old disused air-raid shelters and naturally we found these irresistible. A few gardens around the corner from us housed two assault courses we called the Wee Sui and the Big Sui. Sui was short for suicide and they were pretty well named. The back gardens, or courts as we called them, were divided by walls and had air-raid shelters next to the middens, which was the place where you put your rubbish out.* The challenge was to run along the walls and jump between the shelters.

The Wee Sui was a five-foot jump from a big air-raid shelter onto a smaller one and the Big Sui was a huge leap from a shelter into a midden. Once I saw a guy with studs in his boots do it. He landed and went flying off the end, and it terrified me forever out of doing it. I've often told people that I jumped the Big Sui – in fact, I even told Pamela once, trying to impress her! – but the truth is I never had the balls to do it. I did the Wee Sui but even then, I landed with my toes on the edge, slipped off and had to have stitches under my chin.

I tried to find things to do with myself. I joined the Wolf Cubs and promised to dyb-dyb-dyb do my best. Akela – an upper-class woman from up the road called Mrs Lamont – divided us into groups of six, marked by colours, and put me into the grey six. I was a wee bit pissed off as I wanted to be in red. This was nothing compared to my mental grief when I graduated to the Scouts. We

---

* If a kid said, 'He's got a face like a midden,' it wasn't very complimentary. It meant they had bad acne. Or we'd say: 'Don't squander your money buying a wig. Glue your head, and dive into a barber's midden!' We kids used to go find women's stockings and bean cans in the midden. We'd fill the can with ashes from the fire, put it in the stockings and swing it around like a weapon.

were all divided into patrols again and I really fancied being a Wolf or a Buffalo. I can't say that I was best pleased at being made a fucking Peewit.

The Scouts would go door to door doing bob-a-job, polishing shoes and tidying gardens. I couldn't help noticing the same thing that struck me when I went around friends' homes after school: other people's houses always seemed happier, friendlier and more relaxed than mine.

Although I hated school, I loved reading. I joined the local library in Partick and used to go down, firstly with Florence and then on my own. I would read anything and everything, from Enid Blyton and *Just William* to books on history and war planes. It engendered in me a love of literature that has stayed with me through life. I was also mad keen about playing football in the street. We would kick a tennis ball around for hours. Everybody did, back in the Fifties – it was why Scotland always had such great football players. Sadly, that is very much not the case nowadays. I started playing for a team, St Benedict's Boys Guild. I was an outside right and loved it, even though I wasn't a natural, talented football player. In fact, let's cut the crap here; I was absolutely shite, but I was very enthusiastic.

When I was about seven, my dad took me to my first football match. It was Celtic, of course. Celtic was my dad's team, and my uncles', and when you are that age, your dad knows everything and is always right. I suppose kids who supported Rangers thought that their dads knew everything, as well – but my dad knew more than theirs. So Celtic it was. Oddly enough I can't remember the score of the first game I saw, but I remember that it was Celtic versus Forfar Athletic and I absolutely loved it. I couldn't believe how many people were there – 50,000? 60,000? – and I found the whole experience amazing.

I loved the night games, under the floodlights, the most. I remember once going into Parkhead with my dad and hearing a woman behind me say to the man she was with, 'Oh, you didn't tell me that it was in colour!' It sounded ridiculous but, in a funny way, I knew exactly what she meant.

In my mind now, Celtic won every game I ever saw them play, which may come back to the thing of me being an irrational optimist. I had a couple of favourite players. We had a giant winger from Northern Ireland called Charlie Tully, who would do things like sit on the ball. He was a delight to watch. I also loved our centre forward, John McPhail. I remember watching him once as he was careering up the wing, and as he was running he went up his sleeve and got his hanky out to blow his nose. I liked that he didn't tuck it back in again afterwards.

Given the bollocks I was going through at school, it was no surprise to anybody, least of all me, when I failed my eleven-plus. I had to try again and just about managed to get into St Gerard's Secondary School in Govan. This place was a definite improvement on St Peter's and Big Rosie, but, there again, I can't think of too many places on the planet that wouldn't have been. It even had a uniform: a green tie and green blazer with the school badge on the pocket. I remember the motto was *Sursum corda*: lift up your hearts. It lifted up mine a wee bit and I even managed to marginally improve my academic performance, initially. In my first year I came tenth out of about thirty boys, which I thought was pretty brilliant. But I still didn't really see the point of it all and I soon slid away again.

The violence wasn't as bad as in my primary school but it still went on. A maths teacher, Mr Campbell, had a thin leather belt he called Pythagoras to hit the kids with. One day my cousin, John, snuck in and stole it, cut it up into tiny pieces and left it in the drawer for the teacher to find. A few days later, Mr Campbell produced a new belt with 'Pythagoras 2' written on it, whacked it on his desk and said, 'Who'd like to try it out?' It's a sign of how fucked up everything was back then that the whole class put their hands up and we all took it in turns to sample the new strap.

I used to get the subway from Partick under the Clyde to Govan and then get the electric tram, or caurs as we called them, the last half a mile to school. I loved those trams and they are totally and ineffably bound up with my memories of my Glasgow boyhood. The trams were the main and the best way to get around Glasgow and I was on them every day. Any time you went down to any main road you would always be able to see one trundling along towards you, in the distance. They didn't go very fast so even if it was ahead of you, you'd still be able to chase and catch it. The caurs had a peculiar, electric smell that I will never forget. They smelled like hot metal.

We'd go from Govan Cross to my school. I remember one of my pals, Phil Moore, used to have his books tied with a belt that he slung over his shoulder, and he'd go all the way to school hanging off the back of the tram and kicking his books. They went at just the right speed for that sort of thing.

The caurs were the same at both ends. There was a driving cab at the front and back. The driver would get to the terminus and walk to the other end of the bus to drive it back. As he went through the carriage, he would flip all of the seats so they faced the other way. We never paid a fare. There were stairs at both ends of the bus, so as the conductor went up the stairs at the front, we'd nip down the ones at the back.

We were taking our lives in our hands by doing that, mind, because you wouldn't want to get caught out fare-dodging. A few of the conductors were men, but most of them were women. They took no shit and were scared of nobody. They bossed those trams. The conductresses' famous cry was, 'Come on, you, get off the bus!' It sounded like they were yelling, 'Come on, get off!' There was even a funny song about them:

> *Mary McDougal frae Auchenshuggle*
> *The caur conductress!*
> *Fares please, fares please . . .*

Some trams would go to Auchenshuggle but I've never met anybody who knows where or what the fuck it was. It was one of those places that was just a point on a map – it wasn't a town, or anything. It only existed as a tram stop.

The conductresses were lippy and they took the piss out of the passengers mercilessly. They had an answer for everything:

'Does this tram stop at the Renfrew ferry?'

'I hope so, it cannae swim!'

'Excuse me, does this caur go to Milngavie?'

'No, it doesnae.'

'Well, it says Milngavie on the front!'

'It says India on the tyres and we're not going there, either!'

Milngavie was a way outside of Glasgow and that was a brilliant thing about the trams – they went right out into the countryside, as far as Loch Lomond. Once a year, Dad would take me and Florence out there for a day trip for our annual curious gawp at nature.

We'd get a caur to the movie theatre sometimes. I used to go to a cinema called the Western, which was well named as Westerns were what I mostly watched there. We used to cheer the Indians against the cowboys, because they were the underdogs and they had the best horses.

I also went to the ABC and joined up with a fine wee body of boys and girls called the ABC Minors. They would show us a movie on a Saturday morning followed by a *Flash Gordon* serial.

They would make us sing for our supper beforehand. A bouncing ball on screen would show us the words:

> *We like to laugh and have a sing-song*
> *Such a happy crowd are we*
> *And we're all pals together*
> *The minors of the ABC!*

After *Flash Gordon* they'd play the national anthem. There used to be a monitor, a little fascist with an armband, who tried to make you stand for 'God Save the Queen'. Everyone ignored him and there'd be a dirty great rush for the door, with kids pulling each other back to get out first as if somebody had shouted 'Fire!' The ABC decided that they couldn't have that rampant disrespect for the monarch and moved 'God Save the Queen' to the middle of the show. So now you had to stand and sing the national anthem if you wanted to see *Flash Gordon* and not get kicked out into the street.

No trip into town was complete for me without paying a visit to Tam Shepherd's Trick Shop in Queen Street. It purveyed practical jokes and high-quality fake vomit and dogshit to the children of Glasgow. It still does: the shop has been in the same place for 130 years.

Tam himself was running the place then and he was a put-upon soul. He often seemed a wee bit fed up and, thinking about it, maybe he had good reason to be. The big thing with me and my mates was to open the shop door, lean in and shout, 'Hey, Tam, how's tricks?' The joke may have been palling on him by the thousandth rendition.

Tam had lines of recalcitrant youth buying problems for the world in his shop. It had a glass counter with, for some reason, a two-bob piece glued to the underside. Kids would say it was theirs, pretend they had put it down, and try to use his own money to pay him. Tam would wearily shake his head, 'No, son, that's nae gonna work.'

He sold ridiculously good stink bombs and I was a very enthusiastic purchaser of them. They were glass bulbs with yellow liquid in them. Me and my friends would set them off on the bus or the tram to school. We would go into the train toilet, fasten a stink bomb to the underside of the seat with black adhesive tape and gently put it back down. Then we'd wait for a passenger to go in, drop his pants and squat, at which point a truly rancid smell and a pissed-off voice would waft through the bog door:

'Oh, for fuck's sake!'

Everybody in Glasgow loved the caurs – they were a huge part of the city. It felt like they were pals of ours. When the council said they were putting an end to them and taking them out of service at the start of the Sixties, the general public were dead against it. The council didn't listen and they replaced them with buses, which are just as disruptive to traffic and cause a lot more environmental grief. It was a big con. Today people realise that having electric trams in your city is a real asset and worth the money, but it is too late now for Glasgow – they're long gone.

Years later, I was in Hong Kong and I saw that they had got the old Glasgow caurs working out there. They were the exact same trams. It was wonderful to see them again. I took photos of them and had them framed. My daughter has one on her wall.

As Florence and I grew up and got into our teens, Mona and Margaret's tiny flat in Partick felt even more crowded with so many people squashed into it. So, when I was fourteen we thought it was great when we benefited from a new Glasgow council housing strategy. Due to overcrowding and their general worn-down state, the council wanted to knock down some city centre tenements and reduce the occupation levels of others, including our place in Stewartville Street. We got transferred to a house in Drumchapel, eight miles west of the city. It seemed an excellent move at first. Instead of a cramped tenement we now had a three-bedroom house. It meant Florence and I could share a bedroom and we didn't have to sleep in with our dad and aunties any more.

I knew that the English always said 'two-up, two-down' about houses in a snotty, dismissive way, but I had always imagined that it must be the height of absolute luxury to have stairs in your house. *I mean, stairs! In your house!* Now, we even had a bath! I had my first ever shower at fourteen years old.

Where Partick had been all tenements, now we had some green

land around us. We got given bits of garden, and I learned how to grow potatoes and primulas. There was even a lovely copse nearby called Bluebell Wood where we romped, swinging in trees, picking bluebells and chasing rabbits.

Drumchapel seemed like a promised land at first . . . but then the scales began to fall from our eyes. We started to feel very cheated. Because there were houses there but there was fuck-all else. There were no amenities whatsoever: no shops, cafés, pubs, cinemas, not even any churches. Nothing.

Drumchapel was just outside Glasgow – or, rather, it was near Glasgow and just outside civilisation. It was weird. There was nowhere to buy groceries. If we needed bread, or tea, we had to wait for little green vans that operated as mobile shops to call around once a day. We'd avidly listen out for them in the same way that kids listen for ice-cream vans: 'Doo-da-loo-da-loo-da-loo!'

It was a crime to move thousands of people to a remote housing estate with nothing there except houses. In fact, Glasgow Council made the exact same stupid mistake with two estates to the south-east of the city, Easterhouse and Castlemilk. The weird thing was, they had got it right before, in Knightswood, where they had given the people facilities. They had planned it out properly there, but when it came to Drumchapel, they fucked it up.

We had nowhere to go or to let go of our emotions. We boys would gather in little gangs and just wander around the streets. We weren't looking for mischief – we were looking for something, *anything*, to do, before we gave up and all went off to bed.

I can still get pissed off whenever I think about Drumchapel. Even as a boy, it was obvious to me that things like cafés, cinemas and theatres are essential to a sane and normal life. If you live in a town with none of those things, a dullness descends on the place and an anger develops among the people. It felt like the council had played a dirty trick on us. It was as if they thought that all we people were good for was to go to work, come back home to our houses and quietly watch TV until we died. To me, it was a nasty way of thinking and it showed a real contempt for us. I think that it would be a very good idea to make town planners live in the places that they plan. However, in my experience, you tend to find that the people who plan fuck-ups like Drumchapel usually reside in nice Georgian terraces.

Having, at least, moved up the housing ladder from a tenement to a pebble-dashed terrace, my family developed a weird social snobbery. We lived in a street named Kinfauns Drive and fancied ourselves to be somewhat superior to our neighbours who lived across the way, in a street that led off our road, called Pilton Road. We had been switched from Stewartville Street because the council wanted to reduce the number of people living in our block, whereas the Pilton Road residents had been moved because their entire tenements were being demolished. They were thus technically 'slum clearance' people, which was the charming phrase that we applied to them.

I had to admit, though, that they normally seemed to be enjoying themselves a lot more than we were. With no pubs in

Drumchapel to go to, they would throw rowdy house parties on most Friday nights, and Florence and I would lie in bed and convulse with laughter at the noises coming through our window. The parties would always start off in jolly style, with happy chattering and bursts of somebody playing the accordion and raucous singing. It would never be long, though, until something kicked off and the tone changed markedly.

'Hey, you! What did you fucking say?'

'Nothing! And what's it to you, anyway?'

'*Get tae fuck!* I'll have ye . . .'

Somebody would yell 'Stop the band!', the accordion would groan to a halt and there would be the unmistakable sound of loads of pissed people knocking shit out of one another. The fight would get broken up, the main culprit chucked into the street and the door slammed behind him: 'And don't come back!'

'You can stick your fucking party up your arse!' the guest would advise his hosts before staggering off up Pilton Road, attempting to master 'That's Amore' like a sloshed Caledonian Dean Martin. Life over at slum clearance seemed fun.

One of the many things the planners had not given us was schools, so I carried on going to St Gerard's in Govan. I was herded on to a bus each morning and shipped eight miles back into Glasgow, along with every other kid from the estate. But it was another form of transport that was to provide my physical and mental escape from Drumchapel.

My dad gave me a second-hand bike, a purple New Hudson, and I got really serious about cycling. I was hugely into it. I even had a cycling outfit. I had the shorts, and my grandfather gave me my uncle's ancient cycling top with the name of a local bike team, the Glenmarnock Wheelers, on the front. It was all moth-eaten but I loved it.

I would ride good distances, off to Dunoon and Gourock and places like that. I would easily do fifty miles at a time. I thought cycling was great – it was free transport, and it got me away for a few hours from Drumchapel and housing estates and my aunts. I never joined any cycling clubs or anything like that. Instead, I'd just join in with big bunches of cyclists as they went along. They used to call me a 'gringo' – I liked that because it made me sound like an outlaw. Or I would go on my own, from Glasgow through the hills to Dunoon, across the Clyde on the ferry and back the southern way. It would take me the whole day.

When I was fourteen or so I'd get together with two or three schoolfriends and we'd go off on our bikes, camping. We'd just grab our tents and ground sheets and a few tins of soup and bottles of water and off we'd go, away for the weekend to Bowling or Balloch or up to Loch Lomond. I'd tell my father I was going camping for the weekend but he'd have no idea where I'd gone. If somebody were to ask him where I was, he wouldn't have had a clue. Parents today wouldn't dream of allowing their kids that freedom. They'd go crazy at the very notion: 'But the trees are full of paedophiles who will drop on my child as he cycles along!' I think that's a big shame.

Kids nowadays go out on their bicycles looking like fucking medieval lancers. You see a boy on a small scooter going along the pavement with his mother and he's got a big helmet on as if he's in the Tour de France. Does she think he's going to plummet from his scooter to the ground and break his skull?! To me, it's all overdone. Kids don't need helmets, or armour. You fall off your bike, you skin your knee, and you don't do it twice. Kids have to have the chance to learn.

I was growing up, and I took my first steps into the world of paid employment while I was living in Drumchapel. I had some friends who used to work for a local dairy on the early-morning milk round. They got paid £1.50 a week for doing it, which sounded a small fortune to me, and they managed to get me onto a round.

It was a seriously early start in the mornings and my dad would wake me up at 4 a.m. and make me porridge for breakfast. My father was always great at waking up. He'd never set an alarm – he'd just tell his mind what time he needed to wake up and wake up then. The only time he ever overslept was years later, when I bought him a Goblin Teasmade, which was the absolute height of futuristic sophistication in Scotland at the time. Dad slept right through it.

I would cycle a mile across a frozen field to meet the milk float at a farm in the next village, Bearsden. The milk boys' first job was to milk the cows and they taught us how to do it. You sat on a stool, side-on to the cow, got your knees underneath her, laid your head against her side and gently worked the milk out.*

Naturally, I soon worked out a trick of how to zap the other lads with the milk from an udder. You had to hide behind a cow, wait for your mate to wander over and then whip off the safety catch and blast them in the face:

> *'Pssst!'*
>
> *'Ahh, you bastard!'*

I thought that this was absolutely hilarious.

The milk round itself lasted for an hour or so and it was proper hard work. The milkmen worked us to death. The milk float would never stop, so you had to jump off holding a crate with a handle, with six or eight bottles of milk in it. You'd run to the houses, deliver your milk, then have to chase after the float with the empties in the crate, jump on it and refill the crate. It was lucky my cycling had made me as fit as a flea. We had to be like Greek athletes.

---

* I have seen truly wonderful photos from this era of Scottish farmers milking Highland cattle, which are so robust and sturdy that even the females have huge horns. Before they milked them, the farmers took off their wellies and put them on the cows' horns, so that the animals couldn't suddenly turn their heads and stab them to death.

We delivered in Drumchapel and in Bearsden, which was a more upper-middle-class area where the people had bottles of cream as well as milk. One old estate had gates at the entrance named the Girnin Gates. Girnin means 'crying' in Scottish, and I always wondered if they were called that because they made a squeaky noise like crying when we opened them.

Two footballers lived on our round, in the posh bit of Bearsden: Bobby Evans, the Celtic right-half, and Willie Waddell, the legendary Rangers forward who was later to go on to manage them. I never met them, because the float driver always knocked the doors and collected the money himself, but I was sorely tempted more than once to piss in Willie's gold-top.

One time we had a thief on the round, stealing milk from one of the doorsteps in Ladyloan Avenue. Alec, the milkman I was working with, had a brainwave, and told the guy who lived there, 'When we deliver your milk tomorrow, don't take it in – let it be stolen.' Alec doctored the milk with a very high-powered laxative. There were no more milk thefts.

Winter mornings were freezing cold and I loved hanging on the back of the float and being pulled through the snow on the estates. The delivery lads threw snowballs at each other. One morning, I was running along carrying two empty bottles and ducking to avoid the snowballs being wanged in my direction. As I jumped over the fence between two houses my toes caught on top of it. I crashed to the ground and one of the bottles smashed and burst a tendon in my hand. It hurt like hell and the local hospital had to do a transplant operation and take a tendon out of one of my toes to replace it. So that was the end of my milk-boy days, but doing that job was great for me. It taught me about work, earning money and standing on your own two feet. I think it's a very good thing for teenagers to do as they stop being children and head tentatively into adulthood.*

My tendon injury also meant that I was away from St Gerard's for a few weeks but I can't pretend that that was the sole reason for my woeful academic performance. I had always endured school rather than enjoyed it and when I left with nothing more than a couple of engineering certificates, that seemed about right. I was delighted to leave: I can still remember walking out the gates of St Gerard's at fifteen-and-a-half and, under my breath, saying to myself, 'Don't. Look. Back. Don't. Look. Back.' And I never have.

The shipyards were calling me by now and my mind was getting set on a career in engineering but I did a couple of jobs to fill the time as I waited to be old enough to start there. That was a good thing about Glasgow in the late Fifties – we had full employment and it was rarely a problem to find a job.

I began work as a messenger boy at John Smith's bookstore on St Vincent Street in the middle of the city. Sitting killing time in

---

* Many decades later, I was introduced to Mark Knopfler from Dire Straits at an event and we started chatting. Mark told me he was from Glasgow and had lived in Bearsden until he was about seven years old. 'My God!' I told him. 'I can remember your name from my milk round!'

the shop between making my deliveries gave me a chance to do some reading, and that was where I formed a hearty appreciation of both Nevil Shute novels such as *A Town Called Alice*, and the Scottish national poet, Robert Burns. Mostly, though, I was out on the road, delivering parcels of books to people's houses, and magazines and papers to accountants and lawyers. I would take periodicals to John Grierson, the Scottish filmmaker who is credited with changing the face of documentary films – in fact, they say he even invented the word 'documentary'. Grierson had made marvellous documentaries such as *Night Mail*, which followed the London, Midland and Scottish Railway nightly postal train from London to Glasgow. 'Hello, son,' he used to say to me on his doorstep. 'So, what are you going to make of yourself?' It was a fair question, but I didn't really have much of an answer.

I thought it was OK at John Smith's but I wasn't there for long before I got fired. Some guys in the dispatch department had a scam going whereby they were throwing perfectly good books into a dustbin by the back door, claiming they were damaged, then picking them back out of the bin after work and flogging them. I knew nothing whatsoever about this heinous skulduggery but for some reason I got scapegoated and blamed for it. I tried to protest my innocence to the manager sent to fire me, but he was having none of it: 'I'm afraid you will have to go, Mr Connolly.'

Next, I fetched up as a van boy doing deliveries for a company called Bilsland's Bakery in Anderston. You might have thought they'd be a wee bit concerned about hiring a delivery boy who had recently been fired from a similar job for alleged thieving, but my dodgy CV never came up. They couldn't care less what I had been up to.

I was out on the road with a driver delivering bread and cakes from the bakery to the shops dotted around Glasgow and Paisley and out on the way to Edinburgh. For a while my driver was a guy called Tony Roper. Tony was slick: he had sideburns, wore drainpipe trousers and shortened his bakery coat to make him look even more like a Teddy boy. Like the impressionable wee boy that I was, I admired him. Tony and I zoomed around in a Bilsland's van, drank tea out of jam jars and helped ourselves to bread and cakes from delivery boxes. We'd burst a box open and claim it had got 'shanned', or damaged.*

The delivery coats were to give Bilsland's some grief. Some clot of a manager decreed that the company's brown bakery jackets were to be phased out and replaced by green ones fastened with a yellow half-belt. This was greeted with delight by the Celtic-supporting workers, who could now proudly wear their team's colours. Rangers fans refused to put them on and stuck with their old brown coats.

The Bilsland's job was fun for a few weeks but an ambitious wee boy can only get so much satisfaction out of shanned boxes,

---

* Tony was very funny and went on to be a famous Scottish TV writer and actor in shows like *The Steamie* and *Rab C. Nesbitt*. We kept in touch: four years ago, I wrote the foreword to his autobiography.

white sliced loaves and cream-filled doughnuts. As the clock ticked on towards my sixteenth birthday, I figured that it was time to head off and try to do something major and significant with my young life.

It was time to go and be a welder.

'Go on! Read the Electric Shepherd!'
A Guide to Literature

When I was an unhappy little boy, going to the library changed my life. It may even have saved it. Amazing as it sounds, literature can do that for you. Books are your ticket to the whole world. They're a free ticket to the entire earth. They're an entry to conversations you wouldn't be privy to otherwise.

People often say that football and boxing are the ways out of the working class and they are your ticket out of *that kind of life*, if you happen to want to leave it. But, for me, the library is the key. That is where the escape tunnel is. All of the knowledge in the world is there. The great brains of the world are at your fingertips.

With my aunt making my life hell and Big Rosie beating the shit out of me on a daily basis, I lived in a dark and forbidding world as a kid. But I only had to leave our home and walk over the tramlines to Partick Library and a whole new world opened to me. Reading books showed me that there was something better, *something other*, out there. It made me realise that, despite the constant misery of my day-to-day existence, the world might actually be a good place, and an exciting one.

Partick Library was heaven. When you walked in the door the library was on the left and on the right was a newspaper section. They had the newspapers, on sticks, ready to be read in an upright position. Old men used to come in to read the papers in the warm. There was a wonderful atmosphere of the old guys reading the papers and looking for somebody to talk to, and young guys darting about and having a laugh. Partick Library was a lovely place to be. I'm so glad it's still there today.

A world opened up inside four walls: Partick Library

I can still remember joining the library, being given my little member's card and being all proud, and being led over to the children's section. There were books that I have never seen since, such as *Cowboys Cowboys Cowboys* and *Pirates Pirates Pirates*. You were allowed to take one home to read and bring it back a week later, and it felt such a privilege to be allowed to read a library book at home.

I loved everything about the library. It would be a big social event. I'd meet up with my friends in there and we'd consult about the books:

'Have you read *Cowboys Cowboys Cowboys*?'

'No, but I've read *Pirates Pirates Pirates*.'

'Oh, I must read that! I'll read *Pirates Pirates Pirates* and you read *Cowboys Cowboys Cowboys* . . .'

When you got to twelve years old, you went up a grade in the library system and you were allowed to take *two* books a week home. I remember swanning up the street with my two books, hoping that somebody would see me. I was in the big league now – *two books!* – and I got moved to a different section of the library. There was more sophisticated reading matter there, like *Seven Years in Tibet*, which fascinated me – Tibet sounded so remote, like it was on a different planet.

My love of literature has stayed with me through life. I don't go to libraries so much any more but I love bookshops. One of the things you can do in a bookshop that you can't do buying books online is you can put your nose in a book and smell it. Once you have got the smell of books, your heart races and you are hooked for life. Oddly, Bibles tend to smell pretty good.

There is a town called Wigtown, just east of Stranraer in the Scottish borders. It used to be an agricultural town and not doing too well – the shops were all closing down. But then some bright spark had the idea of holding a book festival there. It happens every September and, during that month, the population of the town rockets from 900 to 12,000. Some people now know Wigtown as Booktown. That makes me very happy.

If you'll allow me to climb on my wee soapbox here, reading books is wonderful. They even make you sleep well. Not electronic books and Kindles and all that shite: they will keep you awake. They mess with your eyes. I'm talking about regular, paper books. Start reading one at night when you go to bed and you will inevitably nod off and wake up with the book on your chest, your light still on, and one leg out of the bed. God knows how many times I have done that over the years.

You must never stop reading books, even if the way that you read changes over the years. Somebody recently showed me a quiz called 'What Kind of Reader Are You?' Now, I don't know about you, but I can recognise myself at various points in my life in these different archetypes:

- **The Polygamist Reader** – this is a multi-task reader who loves reading a load of books at a time and somehow manages never to muddle up the stories. I used to be like that. I would have books on the go all around the house – one by the bed, one in my jacket pocket, one in the bathroom: all over the place. But I seem to have stopped doing that, over the years.

- **The Monogamous Reader** – the single-task reader who sticks to one book at a time and loves re-reading favourite titles. I have become this guy. I can go back to books because I forget them. I can read a whole book and not remember anybody's name, or what they did – I just remember that I enjoyed it. Some people may see this as a failing but I regard it as a great asset. It's like reading a new book, only it's free!

- **The Extrovert Reader** – an adventurous reader who will grab just about anything filled with words and who loves to explore new books. I was like that for many years, but it's too easy to fall out of the habit.

- **The Introvert Reader** – this is a person who sticks to one genre, identifies with the characters, and analyses and ponders over the plot. He is a man much to be avoided, in my opinion.

- **The Altruist Reader** – someone who tries to help out others and recommends huge reading lists to their friends and family. I used to be this guy, as well.
- **The Neurotic Reader** – this is what I fear I have become. It's the reader who gets easily distracted, switches between books and, as a consequence, hardly ever finishes a book. I have got half-finished stuff lying all over the place.

But there's no right way to read. You are not studying for an exam. The important thing is that books do you good. They improve your life, and the lives of the people around you. They improve *you*. So, assuming you are dying to be given a suggested reading list by an elderly comedian, here are some of the books that, over the years, have made my life better . . .

The Call of the Wild by Jack London

I read *The Call of the Wild* and its companion book, *White Fang*, as a schoolboy. They did me a lot of good. The stories are both narrated by wolves and they tell you of their troubles trying to cope with the human race. After I read *White Fang*, I used to march around Partick imagining I was an intrepid prospector striding through the snowy Canadian wilderness in search of gold.

On the Road by Jack Kerouac

There are some books you should read at a certain age and *On the Road* is one of them. So is *The Dharma Bums*: most Kerouac, in fact.

I read them as a young man, a young hippy, in the Sixties and I was taken with them. But I've tried to reread them later in life and I can't. There is a *trendiness* about them that irritates me, and all that '*I'm trying to find out who I am, man, I'm looking for me!*' crap gets on my tits. But when I was in my late teens and wanting to go travelling and meet girls and smoke dope and stay up all night, those books spoke to me – they offered me a world of possibility that just didn't seem to exist in Partick.

Blandings Castle by P. G. Wodehouse

My father made me read P. G. Wodehouse. That makes it sound like a punishment but it wasnae. I remember the first time I read *Blandings Castle*, I actually fell out of bed from laughing. I was reading about a conman who was pretending to be a missionary, and who was giving a speech about a safari he had supposedly been on. He said, 'I was walking through the longolongo grass when I was set upon by a wild bongobongo. Luckily, I heard the noise of a jongojongo, played by a member of the wongowongo tribe who leapt over the zongozongo . . .' and at about the eighth 'ongo-ongo' word I totally lost it. I was laughing so much that my limbs wouldn't work properly and balance and gravity didn't seem to be the same any more. I slid right onto the floor. Once, I went to Stephen Fry's birthday party and he introduced me to his parents. I said, 'I don't *believe* they are your parents. I think you were written by P. G. Wodehouse.' Stephen said it was one of the greatest compliments he had ever had. If you read Wodehouse it will change you and change your language.

The Adventures of Tom Sawyer by Mark Twain

I'm a huge Mark Twain fan: *The Adventures of Tom Sawyer* and *The Adventures of Huckleberry Finn*. But I tried to read *Tom Sawyer* to my children and I failed. I read it as a child but it is a mistake to think it's a book for children – it is much more sophisticated than that. It was too much for my kids when they were wee, so I waited until they were older and then put them on to it.

Jane Eyre by Charlotte Brontë

When I was a teenager I saw *Jane Eyre* on television, and I immediately read it and then read all of the Brontës. They are such brilliant storytellers. They are great at writing about weather – when you read the Brontës you can *feel* life on the Yorkshire Dales, and the drizzle, and going to church on cold evenings. In actual fact, I went to the Brontës' house in Yorkshire and bought all of their books for my daughters from there, and they absolutely loved them.

Hard Times by Charles Dickens

Dickens was a genius. He's so good to read. You zip through his stuff and you don't know why you are reading so fast, but it's because he serialised his books before he put them out as novels. So, they were written as a series, just like those serials you used to get in the cinema – *don't forget to look in next week!* They have cliffhangers and a great fast dynamic so that is how you read them.

Dubliners by James Joyce

James Joyce frightens a lot of people mainly because of *Ulysses*. They think it makes them look unintelligent because they cannae read it. But somebody in Ireland once explained it to me. They said, 'Most books are *about* something; *Ulysses is* something.' Once you get that into your head, it all makes more sense. It's a book that you can just plunge into at any place, because it doesn't go logically from one to ten. It just ambles around. I remember sitting up in bed and reading it and loving having my brain thrown around by James Joyce. *Dubliners* is a collection of early short stories of Dublin and is one of the 'easier' Joyce books, but it's still great stuff.

Crime and Punishment by Fyodor Dostoyevsky

The Brothers Karamazov and *Crime and Punishment* by Dostoyevsky are two excellent books about murder and different ways of looking at it and dealing with it. I devoured all that I could of Dostoyevsky, which was a lot. You mustn't be scared by the size of his books, just treat each of them like a series. If it was a television series in sixteen episodes you wouldn't say, 'Oh God, that's too long!', you'd just get on with watching it. In fact, that's true of all the great Russian authors. Don't be put off by the size of the Russians! A novel like Tolstoy's *War and Peace* is – let me use a technical term here – a big bugger, but you'll get into it and it'll pay you back. Or Nikolai Gogol – there is a Russian that nobody talks about. He wrote mainly short stories, like *The Overcoat*, and they are very funny.

The Master and Margarita by Mikhail Bulgakov

Here's another great Russian novel. Many years ago, I was looking for one of Dostoyevsky's books and went to a bookstore on Princes Street in Edinburgh. They didn't have it but the woman in the shop recommended this. It's a book about the Devil coming to Russia and is a very thinly disguised allegory about Stalin and his reign of terror. Now, that may sound dry as dust to you but it's absolutely brilliant, a colossal book.

A Confederacy of Duncos by John Kennedy Toole

This is probably my favourite book of all time. I've read it so many times and I still go back to it today. It's set in New Orleans and it's the story of a grotesque waster named Ignatius J. Reilly. It's weird and a bit surreal and it stays with you long after you have read it – for your whole life, in fact. It's the only book that John Kennedy Toole wrote. He committed suicide, and some people say that it was because he couldn't get A Confederacy of Dunces published, but who knows if that is true? His mother got it published after his death. One of the loveliest

things that you can do for a person is give them a book that you have enjoyed, and I've given away more copies of this than any other book. In fact, I once went into a local bookstore and said to an assistant, 'Oh, I'm glad to see you that have got a few copies of A Confederacy of Dunces.' She said, 'They are for you!' I had bought so many copies from the shop to give to friends that they had ordered extra stock in just for me.

But this is a book about being made in Scotland, so I have saved up a couple of my very favourite Scottish writers until the end – two people that, if you have never investigated, you should certainly do so as soon as you have finished this sentence. Or maybe this one. What, are you still here? What the hell are you waiting for?

The Complete Poems and Songs of Robert Burns

When I was working in John Smith's bookstore in Glasgow as a spotty teenager, one of my duties was to sweep the floor each morning. I would be the only person in the bookshop, which was a great luxury, and I would scour all the books. I found a wee book of Rabbie Burns' poems and it kind of changed my life. I best remember one called 'To a Louse', which Burns wrote on seeing a louse on a woman's neck in church: '*I fear ye dine but sparely/On sic' a place.*' It made me laugh out loud. Burns gave me back a love of Scottish words that I knew but had dropped, like *sleekit*, which means sly, cunning, sneaky like a fox. I use it to this day: 'Ah, Donald Trump is a *sleekit* man!' Burns' language takes some sorting through, even for me, because he was born on a farm in Ayrshire and some of his rural Scots terms leave me frowning in bafflement. But Robert Burns was a genius. His great poem, 'Tam O'Shanter', is a work of the very highest art. For me, he is Scotland's Shakespeare.

The Private Memoirs and Confessions of a Justified Sinner by James Hogg

Now, here's a character! James Hogg was a shepherd from a village in the Borders called Ettrick. They call him the Ettrick Shepherd. In fact,

I think somebody once called him the Electric Shepherd! I was first attracted to Hogg when I read a quote by him in a bookshop in Inverness. He said, 'I spent most of my youth trying to lose my innocence and succeeded only in finding a higher form of innocence.' I read that and I thought, *Oh, I like you!* It felt like he was writing about me. Because with all the reading I was doing, and the playing instruments, and trying to make something of myself and change my life . . . I wasn't becoming somebody else. I had thought I would become *this other person*, but all I was becoming was a bigger version of what I already was. Hogg wrote this work of genius, *The Private Memoirs and Confessions of a Justified Sinner*, about twins who are desperately unlike each other. You eventually – spoiler alert! – conclude that it is two sides of the same person. It's like Robert Louis Stevenson's *The Strange Case of Dr Jekyll and Mr Hyde* but it came before it. It's a brilliant book – and it was written by a wee shepherd! A few people have tried to make it into a film, and Peter McDougall

Scotland's most literary shepherd: James Hogg

did a good version for TV. James Hogg should be a much bigger figure in Scotland than he is. Everybody goes on about Robert Burns, which is great, but they don't seem to have room to celebrate anybody else, which is a pity. So, go on! Read the Electric Shepherd!

'YOU COULDNAE TACK THE HIGH ROAD!'

When I was a boy, the shipyards dominated Glasgow. They defined the city. Where I lived there was a big, steep hill called Gardner Street. If you stood at the top of it you could look over all of the buildings below and you could see the huge ships. It looked as if the ships were sailing right between the houses. There was this stark industrial beauty to the scene. Ships were lined up right along the Clyde, with workers loading on the whisky and railway engines and all the other things that we exported in those days. It gave the city its heart and soul, and its identity.

I had always assumed I would end up in the shipyards. I did have a vague idea, buried deep within me, that I'd like to be a comedian, but, really, I might as well have wanted to be a fucking astronaut, for how likely it was. In fact, I only ever mentioned it once. My school science teacher, Bill Sheridan, asked me in class: 'Connolly, what are you going to do when you leave school?'

'Sir, I'd like to be a comedian,' I told him. The class erupted in laughter.

'Well, I saw you playing football at lunchtime,' Mr Sheridan told me. 'I think you've already achieved that ambition.'

I did make a half-hearted attempt to join the Army. My father found out and went crazy. Having served in the forces, he thought it would just be a crap way to spend my life and said that I'd be better off as a tradesman. In my heart, I reluctantly agreed with him. That didn't deter me from next trying to sign up for the Navy. My dad went ballistic this time. 'Are you bloody crazy? They're all a bunch of homosexuals!' he raved at me. They had no room for me anyway, so that was the end of my life on the ocean wave.

Really, I just *wanted away*. I wanted to get away from the mundane life I was trapped in: to travel and experience the exciting and exotic outside world the ships were sailing off to each day. But if I couldn't get on the ships and sail, at least I could help to make them.

Most of my pals at school wanted to be marine engineers, and I had done a course in marine engineering, but my engineering career was to take a slightly different path. After I had finished with my delivery jobs for the bookshop and the bakery, I signed up with a shipyard called Alexander Stephen & Sons to be an apprentice welder. Stephen's, as everybody knew it, was a big, thriving yard that built all sorts of ships, from cargo boats to ocean-going liners. Their speciality was prefabrication – making all the constituent parts that could then be assembled and welded together to build the ship.

I was fifteen the day that I walked into Stephen's for the first time, in 1958, and it felt totally exhilarating. I sensed that this was where I would become a man. I was going in as a wee schoolboy with a yodelly voice and I would come out the other end as . . . something else entirely. I'll never forget the noise of that first day. It was so deafeningly loud in there that I thought my ears were going to fall off, and it might even have been a blessing if they had. I felt like turning around and running out of the place just to escape the infernal racket.

The caulkers were making the biggest din. They wielded chisel-like metal-cutters with pneumatic guns at the front and it was their job to make the ships watertight. They were like anti-riveters: where the riveters add metal to the ship, they were cutting it off. I remember one caulker saying, 'I can't hear the noise. I know I make a lot of noise, but I can't hear it when I'm making it.' That would be because every caulker in the yard had made himself stone deaf. You would occasionally hear other workers ask them to leave it off for a minute: 'Eh, caulker, give us a break!'

'Fuck off!' the caulker would cheerily reply.

Starting as an apprentice, I thought there was no way I could survive this constant barrage of deafening noise. Luckily, after a couple of weeks in there, things became a lot easier for me after I suffered permanent hearing damage, just like everybody else. So that was good.

I couldn't begin my apprenticeship until my sixteenth birthday so, at first, I was put to work in the joiners' store, handing out hinges and screws. My boss was a guy called Willie Bain, who only had one leg. He never told me how he had lost the other one and I never asked him.

I did a short stint in the electrical drawing office and then it was time to be an apprentice. There were six of us spotty sixteen-year-olds all gathered together in a tiny wee welding school inside the yard, being instructed by King Farouk of Egypt. Actually, his name was Willie Hughes, but he was a fat, bald little guy with a big moustache, who the other workers reckoned looked like King Farouk, so that was how he went. He was a lovely man who had been captured by the Germans in the war and he had loads of stories about prisoner-of-war camps and what he had got up to in them. He made them sound like a right hoot.

Willie was a brilliant welder and he taught us all the tricks of the trade. We each had little cubbyholes, like confessionals, and every day we would come in and set up these little twelve-inch by four-inch pieces of metal and weld them together at different angles. There we'd be, sparks flying, surrounded by this thump-ing, insane din. It probably sounds totally hellish to a reader today, but I loved it. I had never liked school because I didn't see the point – why the fuck was I learning about Algebra? I was never going to go there! But now I felt like I was employed in doing something that *meant* something: that had a purpose. I was helping to build ships.

The other apprentices were all good Glasgow lads. There was Ginger Brown, and Willy Picket, and Hector Clydesdale. Even at sixteen, Hector was a big strong guy with red hair and a beard, who worked in pubs at nights. He seemed manlier than me, more mature: I was only five foot tall and still felt very boyish. But that was what I loved about the apprenticeship and Stephen's – that I was going to be a tradesman, and be able to make decisions about my own life. And at least I was taller than one of the other apprentices, Christopher Lewis, who we called Wee Lewie.

I've actually stayed in touch with one apprentice, Joe West, for my entire life. Me and Joe are funny. We started school on the same day aged four-and-a-half. We joined the Cubs together, joined the Scouts together, moved to Drumchapel at the same time, and then became apprentices together. The trained, journeyman welders would all walk around the shipyard and when a tradesman needed any welding doing, he would shout over to one of them: 'Hey, welder!' When we were apprentices, nobody shouted to us, so Joe and I would shout it out to each other:

'Hey, welder!'

'Hey, welder!'

Sixty years on, we're still mates. In fact, he came to my sixtieth birthday party. It was great – there were rock stars there, and celebrities, and Prince Charles, and Joe fitted right in. Robin Williams was there and I introduced him to Joe, and said, 'This is my oldest friend.'

'Less of the old,' said Joe.

One day a week, we apprentices would go to college to study for our City & Guilds exams. I'd always figured I was allergic to

classrooms but this was OK because what we were being taught
was related to our jobs – we were learning stuff like metallurgy.
No fucking algebra.

We all wore welders' chaps and rawhide leather jackets to work.
We used to get really hot, as well as getting burned by the welding
a lot. The jackets had buckles that jingled when you walked around,
as if you were a cowboy. I used to sound like Clint Eastwood.

As we got better at the job, we got sent out to do little welding
jobs on the ships as the tradesmen needed us. One day, I put a
washer on the *QE2*. I was passing by and the guy said, 'Hey, welder,
will you do this washer for me?' I thought, 'Oh, great, it's the
QE2!' and I did it.

Many years later I was in Sydney, in a hotel right opposite the
Opera House, and the *QE2* pulled in. I went along and watched all
of the passengers coming off, and I thought to myself, 'I wonder
how my washer is holding up?' It seemed to be doing OK.

For a while I got put to work with a plater and a carpenter
called Bobby Dalgleish and Jimmy Lucas. Their job was putting
the super-structure on the ships, and they were known as the Erection Squad. They were inordinately proud of that name, and what
man wouldn't be?

As well as being an apprentice welder, I used to be the tea boy –
I made the tea for the journeyman welders. There were six of them
and they'd give me five shillings each, which was thirty bob a
week – very nice on top of my £2-6-5d wages. A cup of tea then
was not what a cup of tea is now. There was not a lot of Earl Grey

or ginseng going on. The welders drank black tea, no milk, with four or five sugars, out of Ministry of Food National Dried Milk tins. Tea out of a tin can was better without milk because the can didn't get all black and burned.

I used to love sitting having tea with the welders and listening to them talk. They would talk about anything and everything and it was no holds barred. That was true of all the shipyard workers. As soon as Stephen's doors clanged shut in the mornings, it was a man's world in there – rough, rude, raw and hilarious. Everybody smoked and everybody swore. Every second word was 'fuck'. They talked about work and the factory bosses and football, and amazing, grown-up things like getting pissed and sex. The jokes were furious, nothing was sacred and nothing was taboo. For me, it was heaven.

The funniest men were what we in Glasgow call patter merchants – they had the gift of the gab and would have everybody falling about. I loved those guys. I have no doubt that that is what my comedy first grew out of – trying to do the same thing of telling stories and riffing away. Trying to be a patter merchant.

The patter merchants were always very observant about each other. If you showed any weakness, such as if you were keen on anything outside of their realm, they would crucify you for it.

There's a Scottish word 'birl', which means spin. If you're spinning, you are birling. It was used for being drunk sometimes: 'Oh, he's birling.' One guy who was hardly ever drunk was Johnny, a welder from Troon, who was working on an oil tanker, who used to drink tea with us. He was different from everybody else, being a country boy from Ayrshire, and the men took the piss out of his accent mercilessly. Johnny was a bit of an amateur dancer and one day one of the welders spotted him practising at the foot of the tanker when he had a minute to himself. The welder went over to talk to him.

'I saw you having a wee dance, there?' he asked him.

'Aye,' said Johnny. 'I was practising a reverse birl.'

From that moment on Johnny was the Reverse Birler to the whole yard. 'Hey, Reverse!' people would say, and he had no choice but to answer to it. I've no idea if he minded, but he probably knew that if he showed it upset him, the men would do it all the more.

Some of the other men were just good at telling jokes. There was one well-known guy called Pig McCrindle. He got called that because, well, he looked like a pig. Everybody on the Clyde knew Pig – he used to get on stage at the trade union meetings and tell jokes. They were just old-fashioned gags, about Englishmen, Scotsmen and Irishmen walking into bars, or a man walking into a bar with a crocodile on a leash. That kind of stuff. I always thought that I wanted to find that wee bar. It sounded fun.

The tradesmen at Stephen's had insults for the other trades. If a plater cocked up on a job, he would get told, 'You couldnae plate soup!' If you wanted to wind up a joiner, you told him, 'You couldnae join hands at Hogmanay!' An electrician who failed to get things working was informed, 'You couldnae get juice out of a

Jaffa!' And as we welders used to tack, we'd get, 'You couldnae tack the high road!'

I was proud of being a welder. I knew that when my apprenticeship ended, welders were the highest paid of all the tradesmen. Welders always had a few bob in their pockets. There was a joke about this on the Clyde: 'Two guys are walking down the street. One of them is drunk and the other one is a welder, too.'

One day in 1961, all of the apprentices from every yard on the Clyde were given the afternoon off to go and see a documentary film at the Lyceum picture house in Govan. It was called *Seawards the Great Ships*, and it was all about shipbuilding in Glasgow. It actually went on to win an Oscar the following year.

Everybody settled into their seats, the lights went down, and then a few minutes into the film, the narrator said the fateful line: *'Here are the welders, the kings of prefabrication.'* Hooray! All of us welders let out a huge roar, which didn't go down well with some of the other apprentices.

'Eh? Fucking rubbish!'

'What? Who are you fucking talking to?'

Someone took a swing at someone and a big battle broke out in the cinema: they had to put the lights up to subdue it. But the movie was right: we *were* the kings of prefabrication.

I was proud watching that film . . . but I was also suspicious of it. Like most things that came out of England, or more specifically London, about Scotland, it felt patronising: those la-di-da cut-glass accents talking about '*the Scotsman, brave, bold and true*' like we were some kind of fucking exhibit. It was a long way from our world. It didn't ring true.

Back in Stephen's, we apprentices were getting a wee bit of a bad reputation for playing practical jokes on the tradesman, and we thoroughly deserved it. Wee Lewie usually came up with the bright ideas and he was nothing if not inventive. One of the best ones was giving people electric shocks. When there were rain puddles on an upstairs deck, one apprentice would stand near to a puddle while another one would wait downstairs, right underneath the puddle, holding his welding gear. As soon as somebody walked through the puddle, the apprentice next to it would bang his foot on the deck and the guy downstairs would fire his welding gear against the underside of the deck. It would send an electric shock coursing through the puddle, and the shout from upstairs would tell you it had worked:

'Aaargh! You bastards! I'll break yer fucking necks!'

Then you'd swap places. I loved it, but I can't pretend that it made us all that popular.

Another trick was creeping up behind people and welding the metal horseshoes in the heels of their work boots to the deck. Or we'd paint the heels with the silver paint that we used for highlighting chalk lines. It was really funny seeing these big guys walking away with painted heels, like early glam rockers.

The tradesmen's boiler suits had a little half-belt on the back, and we used to get a welding rod and make it into an S shape. You'd get the paper from your lunchtime cheese sandwiches and hook it on one end of the S, hook the other end over a guy's half-belt, and set fire to it. The poor guy would be walking along, oblivious, with a tail that was on fire.

Come to think of it, health and safety wasn't really a big priority in the Clyde shipyards in the late Fifties.

There again, we apprentices got a fair bit of piss ripped out of us too, as so we should. The welders were particularly fond of sending us off to the stores on nonsensical errands very much at our expense. They'd ask one of us to go get them some tartan paint, and off we'd run only to be met with a gale of mocking laughter when we got to the stores. Or they'd ask us to go for a long stand, and we would be hanging around by the counter for forty-five minutes before the penny dropped.

After I'd been sent for sky hooks, and a bubble for the spirit level, I had had enough and told Willie Hughes to fuck off when he told me to go fetch him some carborundum. This earned me a bollocking from King Farouk as, for once, this one actually did exist: it was a kind of abrasive paste.

As I was growing out of my teens, Stephen's felt like exactly where I was supposed to be. I met the most extraordinary characters in there. I remember going into the blacksmith's shop to dry my gloves, because you'd be pulling a cable around in the rain or the snow and if you had wet gloves, you would get electric shocks.

When I got in the blacksmith's, there was a guy in there working the big steam hammer – THUNK! THUNK! An unholy noise. He had a wire wrapped around his forehead and dangling in front of him, with a lit cigarette in it hanging in front of his mouth. It was his own invention and I thought it was fantastic.

Then there was a guy called Wull the gull. There were always guys in there who were hungrier than everybody else, who would be going around trying to beg sandwiches off people, and Wull was one of them. That was why they called him Wull the gull: 'Dinnae throw your crust away!' they'd say. 'Wull will fly out of the air and grab it!'

There was also a man called Darren Hamilton, who we called Dan the Ham, who was really funny, both when he was trying to be and when he wasn't. He had Tourette's syndrome, and once or twice I'd be working high up on a ship with him, balancing on planks, and Dan would suddenly start jumping about and shouting. I'd have to cling on for dear life: 'What you fucking *doing*, Dan?'

The yard was a man's world apart from the female French pol- ishers, who worked right next to the welding school. Nobody dared mess with them. Somebody told us apprentices that if the women caught one of us, they'd put his dick in a milk bottle and tickle his balls till he got an erection. He'd have to smash the bottle to get it off. We didn't quite believe it, but we didn't quite *not* believe it, either. One morning a couple of the French polisher women were running past the welders' store. They were late for clocking in. One of the welders, a big, funny guy named Cammy, yelled over to them: 'Don't run, dears, you'll heat your water!'

Without missing a beat, a polisher turned around and told Cammy, 'Well, you won't be scalding *your* cock in it!' She remains engraved in my memory. Just the kind of girl you'd like to take home to Mother.

The only other women there worked in the canteen. One blonde tea lady used to fascinate me. She always had big love bites on her neck while she was serving the food yet, for reasons known only to her, she would be trying to be posh. Somebody would order mince and she'd say, 'One gent's mince.' Or: 'Two gents' apple pies.' There again, she was a woman of the world. She showed me what the hole in the top of a pie was for by sticking her big painted fingernail through it to check if the pie was still hot.

The shipyard could be a dangerous place and I once fell off a ship. I was on deck and pulling on a cable when it came apart in my hands. I toppled backwards and went right over the edge of the ship. As I began falling, I still remember thinking, *oh fuck!* I fell forty feet and landed feet-first in a wee water-filled coffin-shaped space in between two cranes. I broke my ankle on some scrap metal but it was a miracle that it didn't kill me. They rushed me to hospital and they bandaged it up, sent me home the same day, and I was off work for a few weeks. That was my first ever write-up, in the Glasgow paper: LUCKY BILL FALLS FORTY FEET AND BREAKS ANKLE. All the welders called me Lucky Bill for a while after that. I can't say that I felt all that lucky at the time, hobbling round with a broken ankle.

Employee care was not high on the agenda at Stephen's. I would have to weld in the double-bottom of the ships, using deep pene-tration rods. The thick yellow fumes would turn my lips black. I would stop to go out and have a smoke and the guys working on the pipes in the engine room up above would be snowing asbestos on me. I'd look as if I'd turned grey-haired. It's really quite remark-able I've lived to this huge age.

One day I was working with a carpenter called Coley, doing bits and pieces of welding on a tank for him. I went away to the toilet for a pee, and when I came back there was a bit of nonsense going on around where we had been working. Coley had tripped, fallen into the tank and broken his ankle. They used a crane to lower a stretcher down into the tank and fastened him to it in there before lifting him out, bound up like a mummy, in the way that you see people being rescued from mountains.

As the crane lifted him out of the tank, I asked him, 'Coley, what happened?'

'I was putting a chalk line on the deck and I knelt on my cock,' he told me. I collapsed in helpless laughter on the deck as the crane whipped him away into the sky.

I suppose it was like one big rite of passage in Stephen's and as I got well into my apprenticeship I began to feel less like a nervy boy and more like a man. It helped that I had suddenly had a major growth spurt and wasn't such a midget any more. Suddenly I just felt like there was more of me and I had more about me. When I sat around with the welders at lunchtime or tea breaks, I'd start having the confidence to pipe up a bit and try being a little bit of a patter merchant myself. I had a routine that went down well with Bobby Dalgleish and Jimmy Lucas (a.k.a. the Erection Squad) and with Willie McInnes, who everybody unkindly called Bugsy on account of his protuberant teeth.

My comic turn was impersonating the drunken would-be Dean Martins and Frank Sinatras that Florence and I used to hear staggering home from the late-night parties in Drumchapel: *'When the moon hitsh your eye like a big pizza pie . . . That'sh Amore! Hic.'* I could get them off pretty well. Scots call it gallus singing, and I still sometimes do it in my stage act today.

The managers would sometimes do a tour of the shipyards, in their suits and ties, usually accompanied by the foremen in their overalls with a collar and tie underneath. The managers were pretty aloof figures and we didn't have a lot to do with them if we could help it.

It was so noisy when the whole factory was going that you generally couldn't hear what anybody more than two feet away from you was saying, so the workers used their own sign language to warn each other if a boss was behind them. It was like a rogue strain of Scottish industrial semaphore. If any of us saw a manager coming, we'd pat the top of our head to let everyone know. If it was a foreman, we'd tap three fingers on our upper arm, like a sergeant's three stripes.

There was another bit of sign language that I didn't understand for a while. Whenever anybody wanted to know the time, they would put their hand by their belly and flop it outwards. I used to wonder, *what the fuck is that*? Then I worked out they were miming having a fob watch. If they did it to you, you'd have to try to mime the time back.

At the end of every day the big shipyard hooter would sound and the thousands of tradesmen would all bolt for the exit. There were quite a lot of disabled workers at Stephen's, many wounded in the war, and they went a few minutes before everybody else so they didn't get flattened in the rush. Anybody who happened to be passing the gates as they hobbled out must have thought, 'Jesus! That shipyard is a bloody dangerous place!'

Everybody on the Clyde liked a bevvy. We'd sometimes go to the pub of a Friday lunchtime, and on Mondays everyone would have stories of how they'd been steaming at the weekend – me included. I came a wee bit late to drinking. Through my late teens I was very fit and I was cycling all the time, so drinking didn't interest me. I didn't have my first proper beer until I was about nineteen and away with some friends camping in Troon. We were in a pub called the Portland Arms and I bought a pint. I nearly dropped it – I didn't expect it to be so heavy. But it was lovely drinking the pint and it was the first of many, many more.

Having my shipyard wage meant that in my very late teens, when I first started going out drinking and dancing, I could choose and buy myself some nice clothes for the first time. This felt like a real breakthrough to me and I threw myself into it. We Scots have a phrase, 'going in your own can', for giving your parents some money for housekeeping and being free to spend the rest, and I would give my father £1 per week for my keep then head down to men's fashion stores like the Esquire shirt shop in Glasgow. This was in the days before boutiques were invented.

The Teddy boy era was coming to a close and the Italian style was coming in. So, I would buy American shirts with long, pointed collars, like in the Mafia movies, and a three-button suit with inch vents on the jacket and at the bottom of the trousers. I'd get a short jacket and a tie and hanky to match, and maybe a white shorty raincoat. My shoes would be winklepickers or white moccasins, until I got a pair of basketweave shoes with Cuban heels.

I also gravitated towards pink and bought some pink shirts and pink underwear, much to my father's horror. I will never forget his face when he saw my pink underpants. He thought that I must be turning into some kind of homosexual weirdo and he was absolutely outraged. I thought he was going to have a stroke. Yet the weird thing was that wearing pink made me very popular with the ladies, even as it made me deeply suspect among the men.

Buying my own clothes let me start becoming this thing, this *version of myself* that I had loosely in mind. I wasn't sure what it was yet but I knew I wanted to strike a note when I appeared. When you live on a housing estate with rows of beige houses, like we did in Drumchapel, if you come out dressed up you become a kind of star. I remember one night getting the bus into Glasgow in an Eddie Fisher coat with raglan shoulders that rolled down, and my basketweave shoes with white socks. A woman on the bus looked me up and down and said, 'Aye, you're very neat about the feet.'

'Thank you very much,' I said, and went off to lounge and pose at the back of the bus, feeling like a million bucks, very neat about the feet.

My Saturday nights out in Glasgow started at the Corporation Baths. I would get the bus into town in my going-out clothes and pay half a crown for a lovely deep hot soak in a big metal public bath. I would put my best clothes back on, get myself a shoeshine at Glasgow Central station and then, more often than not, I would head off down to the Saracen Head.

The Sarrie Heid, as everyone knew it – and still does – is on Gallowgate in the heart of Glasgow, over the road from the Barrowland Ballroom and the Barras Market. In the grand old days of the eighteenth century it used to be a stopping inn for the stage-coach to London. It claims to be the oldest pub in Glasgow, and it is definitely the most famous. I am pretty sure the Sarrie is also the only pub in Glasgow that has its own song. It was written by one John Murphy, a great old pal of mine who sadly is no longer with us, and very fine it is, too:

> *The girl that I marry will have to be*
> *Able to swallow more wine than me*
> *And Carlsberg Special Brew*

And Newcastle Brown Ale too
The girl that I marry will drink in the Sarrie with me.

The girl that I marry will have to be
Heiress to a pub or a brewery
I hope she comes on soon
Cause on our honeymoon
The girl that I marry will drink in the Sarrie with me.

In many ways the Sarrie was not the wisest pub to attend in a sharp three-button Italian suit with matching hanky and tie, white shorty raincoat and moccasins. The most popular drink in there was rough cider, or scrumpy. The barman, Angus, was a huge guy who used to pass the pints right over the heads of the people who were leaning on the bar, slopping scrumpy all over them as he did so. My pal Hughie Gilchrist, a Stephen's welder, used to come to the Sarrie and had a novel solution to this problem. He had a Pac-a-Mac, a plastic raincoat that folded into an envelope – a style that swept Scotland – that he used as his drinking coat. He used to keep it in the Sarrie and, whenever he went in, he would put it on and button it up to the neck while he was standing at the bar so that the overhead scrumpy didn't drip on his suit.

The Sarrie's most famous feature used to be a ceramic sherry barrel that stood on a gantry. The little guy who collected the empty glasses from around the bar used to pour the dregs of the drinks in there. When it was full, they would sell you a glass of it.

It was called White Tornado and it was quite a favourite among the customers. It used to drip on to the floor beneath the barrel and I noticed that the drips had eaten a hole in the floorboards. But it wasnae bad.

The Sarrie had a reputation for ferocious roughness and I saw many a fellow being asked to leave and getting oxtered from the premises. In Scotland your oxters are your armpits, and being oxtered from the premises was to be lifted up by your armpits and forcibly dispatched back out the way you came in. Despite that, I don't think I ever saw an actual fight in the Sarrie, despite its fearsome reputation. In fact, this was true of Glasgow as a whole. The city has always had this image of being violent and full of hard men but I'm not sure it is any worse than Liverpool, say, or the East End of London. There was an outbreak of knife crime and razor-slashing in the 1950s but then a judge called Lord Carmont came along and started giving out seven-year sentences for carrying a blade: 'You were walking around with a razor? Seven years!' It stopped it all overnight.

I rarely go in pubs now but I still remember the smells of the Sarrie – the beer, the cigarettes – and I miss them. A thick fog of smoke always hung there. I was the same with smoking as with drinking: I didn't start until I was eighteen or nineteen because of the cycling but once I started, I got really into it. Everyone that I knew smoked. It was everyone at home – except for my sister, Florence, who never did – everyone in Stephen's, everyone in the Sarrie, everyone in Glasgow. It felt like it was *everyone in Scotland.*

There were so many different kinds of cigarette. Domino came in packets of four. If you collected the packets, you could get a set of dominos. Kent, which gave you coupons. Craven A, with a wee black cat on the pack. Du Maurier, in a box. Gold Flake, in a beautiful yellow packet. Sobranie cocktail cigarettes, for the ladies, all pastel shades with gold tips. Sweet Afton had a picture of Robert Burns on the packet with a Burns quote. The lid was a notepad, just in case you were overcome with the desire to write because you were having a fag.*

I will never forget the Sarrie Heid. There wasnae another pub like it in the world. I remember, one night, sitting talking to some women in the wooden snug bar, which looked like a confession box. A hugely optimistic young man with a few rough ciders inside him stuck his head around the corner and said the words that every woman longs to hear: 'Any of ye lasses wanting your hole?' One of the girls hardly even looked up as she asked him, 'Have ye got a motor?' And they say romance is dead.

When I was starting to get a wee bit known in the early

---

* How I eventually stopped smoking is interesting. More than twenty years later I was with Pamela, who suggested, 'It's time you gave up smoking.' I was in a London West End show at the time, and I told her, 'OK. I get 200 Senior Service delivered to my dressing room every Monday. Next week I'll smoke them all, then I'll give up on the Friday.' That Monday, I opened the carton, took out a cigarette and lit it, looked in the mirror and thought, *You're kidding yourself, Billy*. I put it out, gave the 200 fags to the stage doorman, saying, 'Here's a wee pressie for you,' and I never smoked again.

Seventies I went in the Sarrie to shoot some pictures for an LP I had made. I went in and bought a drink. As soon as the photographer came in, the barmen all disappeared under the bar because they thought he was from the social security. I actually went in there again this year, for the first time in maybe forty years, and I was delighted to see it is still a proper pub, not a gentrified semi-restaurant. It's got a collection of knives on display nowadays. You won't see that in many pubs, but that's the Sarrie for ye.

After we had all made our breath stink of scrumpy and cigarettes in the Sarrie, we'd go across the road to the Barrowland to dance. Or, if I am honest, to try and get a lumber, which is what we used to call trying to pull a girl. The Barrowland was – and is – a huge ballroom, and the women used to all stand along the wall and the men stood along the edge of the dance floor. You would try to clock the women and pick one, then have to get your nerve up to walk across the no-man's land to where she was standing and ask that all-important, timeless question: 'Are you dancing?' If the girl told you 'No', all you could do was turn and walk away, mingle back into the crowd of guys and go to another bit of the room to try someone else.

What you should *never* do was say 'OK' to the girl that had turned you down and then ask the girl right next to her. Because you could end up going right down the line . . .

'Are you dancing?'

'No!'

'Are you dancing?'

'No!'

'Are you dancing?'

'No!'

. . . right down the line all the way to the door and away into the street.

I didn't have too bad a success rate at getting the lasses to dance with me – it must have been my three-button shirt and Cuban heels. Sometimes, two women who hadn't been asked to dance, or who didnae fancy the men who had asked them, would dance together, and then you and a pal could go and dance next to them and try to get things going that way. You could try to break them up and get them to dance with you instead.

People were always getting kicked out of Barrowland. More nights than not a fight would break out and the bouncers would just grab whoever was nearest to it: *'Right, you twelve, oot!'* You could easily get caught up in that. I can remember being slung out one night with a bouncer on each side of me. I looked back over my shoulder and saw my feet bouncing down the stairs behind me. The bouncers flung me onto the street in the rain. 'I've got a coat!' I told them. 'Give us your ticket!' they said. I handed them my cloakroom ticket and a bouncer went in, came back out with my shorty white raincoat and – SPLASH! – threw it right into a puddle. 'Ya fucking bastards!' I muttered to myself, as I began trudging back to Partick.

I had some great nights in Barrowland and in the Locarno Ballroom, though. I would leave with a lumber, a wee bit of stuff, and set about trying to get them all the way home. They might live on Easterhouse or Castlemilk, these estates miles from where I lived, and we would be walking for hours. I didnae have a car to take them home, and even when I did get a car as I got a bit older, I wouldn't take it out on a Saturday drinking night.*

On the nights that I didn't get a lumber, I would be heading home on a night bus from George Square. There was often a rammy – a fight – on those buses. I would get on carrying a fish supper and everyone would stare at me because they were starving. I wasn't going to Barrowland so much by the late Sixties when there was a serial killer called Bible John on the loose in Glasgow. He murdered three girls that he picked up in there. The police put out an artist's impression of what he might look like . . . and he looked like me, if I had a Perry Como haircut. They never did catch him.

In the shipyard on a Monday, the older welders would ask me about my nights out and take the piss out of me. 'Are you winchin'?' they'd ask, meaning was I going steady with anyone. I would say, 'Aye, I'm winchin'.' Then they'd ask, 'Has she had you up to see her mother? Have you had the feet under the table and the chocolate biscuits?' That was what you had to do, at that age – go and meet

---

* I'm not sure any girl would have been too impressed with my first car, anyhow. It was a yellow Morris Minor with a vase of flowers on a sticker on the windscreen. The cable from the interior light came down and randomly, mysteriously entered the dashboard. It cost me £40 and was great until it burst into flames as I was driving it.

her parents and get given a cup of tea and a chocolate biscuit while they tried to size you up. Some of the girls' parents were not so keen on me because they thought I was a hairy rascal. I remember having one wee girlfriend and going to meet her mother. They were knitting in the living room together and, to make small talk, I asked the mother, 'What's that you're knitting?' She showed me her knitting pattern. 'What's that mean – K2 tog?' I asked her.

'That's knit two together,' she said. 'You have to watch it because some people . . .' She meant to say, 'Some people are slack knitters,' but she said 'knickers' instead. 'Some people are slack knickers.'

'Oh, aye,' I said. 'I think I've met a couple of them!' The mother didn't speak to me again, and that was the end of me seeing her daughter.

I belonged to Glasgow, and Glasgow belonged to me. It was such a great time of my life, and I had some wonderful nights out, on the town and on the bevvies. I loved beer. I was always a beer drinker until a few years later, when I was out on the road a lot and I got into spirits. My roadie would say, 'This is a brandy tour,' and I would be wolfing down brandies, or 'This is a gin tour.' I would come off stage to a gin and a cigarette waiting for me. It was lovely while I was doing it – but then it was time to stop and I stopped. I stopped drinking while it was still my idea.

I had always been a happy, jolly drunk but it changed, and I became an angry one. The fun went away, and that is the first sign that you are in trouble: the first symptom of having a problem.

I was drinking when I met Pamela, and she soon told me that she couldn't handle me as a nasty drunk and if I didn't stop, she and I would be finished. I knew she was right but, at first, I tried to do the same thing as when I tried to stop smoking. I said, 'Right, I'll give up drinking for a year. A year from today, I'll have my next drink.' I did it. I gave up for a full year, so Pam and I thought everything was fine. On the anniversary we went out for dinner and Pam bought me some Champagne to celebrate. With the first drink, *I was back*. Pam asked me, 'What time is it?' and I said, 'What the fuck is it with you and the time? You're always on about the time . . .' One drink, and I'd become the monster again. So, I quit again. It took me three times but I did it.

It's been thirty-three years now since I last had a drink, and I don't miss it for a second. I was on the Glasgow Cross one morning in spring 2018, at about ten o'clock, and a guy having a fag in the doorway of a pub spotted me and staggered across. Celtic had won the Scottish Cup two days earlier and he was still celebrating. He hadnae been home. 'Eh, Billy, come and have a wee drink with us!' he suggested.

'I've not had a beer in more than thirty years,' I told him.

'Aye, well, you'll be needing one, then!' he said.

I laughed but he couldn't have been more wrong. Drinking is a thing of the past for me now, albeit with many fond memories. Oddly, I don't drink myself, but at dinner I still enjoy smelling other people's drinks. I am lucky that I managed to stop – but a lot of other people weren't so lucky. The tradesmen in the shipyard were always trying to get money for brews. When I think back on it now, a lot of them were deep in alcoholism, but at the time it all seemed completely normal.

Willie McInnes was a lovely guy but he was always drinking away his wages at the weekends and having no money by Monday morning, a practice with which his wife was deeply unimpressed. After one marital tongue-lashing too many, he hit on a plan whereby I could bail him out on a weekly basis.

I was buying a motorbike, a BSA 250, on hire purchase, and had to pay back thirty bob – £1.50 – every week to keep up the payments. Willie knew I was doing this, and one week he came over to me with a proposition.

'That motorbike of yours,' he said. 'How much do you pay for it?'

'£1.50 a week,' I told him. 'But I pay it back monthly – £6.'

'Aye. What do you do – do you take it out of your wages every week and put it aside in a drawer, or something?'

'Aye.'

'Well, I'll tell you what. Instead of doing that, you give it to me and I'll give it back to you at the end of the month.'

So, I basically became Willie's weekly bank. I would give him £1.50 every Monday, and every fourth week he would give me £6 to pay off my motorbike. My bike still got paid off and Willie had a sudden boost in pocket money to get pissed at the weekends.

That was kind of harmless but a lot of the tradesmen would get into money trouble with their drinking. There used to be a grave-yard next door to Stephen's and on Sunday nights there would be two tables set up in the cemetery. One of the tables would be a moneylender, lending the men money at extortionate interest rates. The other table would be a guy selling cheap booze – wine that tasted like vinegar. The workers would get their short-term loans then head straight over to the next table to piss it away.

It was funny to see, in a way, but then again it wasn't. On Friday nights, the moneylenders stood outside the shipyard waiting for the men to come out with their wages and pay them back, with interest. They'd always have a heavy, a hard man, with them to encourage the men to pay up. Hard men get portrayed in dramas today like boxing champion fighters, but these were really nasty, sleazy guys with no morality. They were no friends of the workers.

As I got further into my apprenticeship, and my welding skills got pretty good, I began to work a few weekends. Even better was doing night shifts. You'd work the day, have your sandwiches, and then carry on and do the whole night. The factory was pretty dead at nights but that made a nice change from the usual bedlam, where you couldn't hear yourself think, and I grew to like them. Best of all was what we called the ghoster, where you'd work all day, do the night and then do the following day again.

Ghosters were pretty exhausting, to say the least, but I was young and driven and had bags of energy then, the money was fantastic, and it meant I got these brilliant huge weekends. If I timed it right, I could finish on a Friday morning and not have to clock in again until the Monday night. This was great because as well as big Friday and Saturday nights out in Glasgow, I had joined the Stephen's Apprentice Boys Club and was spending some weekends away with them. We'd go off into the countryside, usually staying in youth hostels. It was good to get out of the city and it was a lot of fun.

I loved it at Stephen's but at the same time I couldn't shake off the feeling that there had to be more to life. I knew that I wanted to . . . *be a somebody*, even if I wasn't totally sure who or what. By the end of my teens I had got heavily into folk music – of which more later – and would daydream about one day playing it myself.

I remember one lunchtime sitting eating my sandwiches on one of the ships, in the propeller shaft. I was gazing down the Clyde and planning what my first album sleeve would look like. What kind of photo of me should I use? Mind you, this was all a wee bit previous as I hadn't even bought a fucking banjo yet.

I kept this private ambition secret from everybody in the yard as I knew they'd only take the piss. Well, from almost everybody. One day I confided in another welder, a guy called Jimmy Duddy, that I wanted to make a record. He stared at me, burst out laughing, and urged me: 'Go on, then! Move like Elvis!'

It's hard to work in a place like Stephen's without developing some kind of political awareness. I wasn't exactly an angry young man but, even so, I looked around me at the poverty and hardship of ordinary people's lives in Glasgow and knew that something, somewhere, in society wasn't right.

As I got into my twenties I also began to experiment with my appearance and to develop the extreme hairiness that I have persisted with until this day. I grew a very long beard, and this hirsuteness, together with my burgeoning political awareness, led some of the men in the yard to christen me Ho Chi Minh.

A few of the lads from work joined the Young Socialists and used to wear a little badge of an arrow pointing to the left. I found them a bit intimidating because they seemed intellectually more together than me so I didn't go to any of the meetings in case I got shown up. But I sympathised with those lads and befriended them.

I became big mates with a shop steward named Willy Adams. We would sometimes go fishing and camping at the weekend on Loch Lomond. Willy was very politically engaged and encouraged me to read books like *The Ragged-Trousered Philanthropists* by Robert Tressell and George Orwell's *Animal Farm*. I got well into Orwell and particularly the romantic nature of his political activism. I loved the fact that he went off to fight in the Spanish Civil War and that his ID card gave his political leanings as anti-fascist. I started telling people that was my politics, too: I was an anti-fascist.

Willy also encouraged me to try to get a scholarship to Ruskin College in Oxford and become a full-time trade union official. I toyed with the idea but it didn't attract me enough, and in any case, I was getting more and more gripped by the idea of playing music.

Willy died towards the end of my apprenticeship, and as long as I live, I will never forget his coffin being driven past the shipyard. All of the men were outside. Everyone wore cloth caps in those days, and as the hearse passed by, they all took their caps off. It looked just like a huge, rolling wave as the whole yard paid its last respects.

Willy opened up a new world of political books to me, yet for all my newfound respect for Orwell and Tressell, my biggest love when it came to books was reserved for P. G. Wodehouse's comic whimsy. I would read Wodehouse avidly at home, devouring the way he used language, and this was to kill any potential political career at work stone dead.

We were in the Boilermakers' Union, but a new trade union named DATA – the Draughtsmen and Allied Technicians' Association – was just starting up for draughtsmen and architect types. They were having trouble being recognised by the management in the shipyards and so wanted to go on strike. They were asking us to back them up.

Our union leaders called a big meeting by the side of the Clyde and it became apparent most of the tradesmen were against supporting DATA. The general mood of the meeting was pretty hostile to the white-collar workers.

'Why should we back them up?' the men were saying. 'They never backed us when we went on strike, they all stayed in and got paid!'

'Aye, fuck those bastards, they just stayed in their offices drinking tea!'

This was going very much against my newfound sense of workers' rights and socialism, so I summoned up all of the courage that I had and put my hand up to speak. Jimmy McPherson, the shop steward who was chairing the meeting, spotted me: 'A-ha, now we're going to hear from Ho Chi Minh! Speak through the chair, brother!'

I was dead nervous but launched into an impassioned address: 'This is desperate and wrong, talking about DATA like this! An attack on them is an attack on trade unionism and on union men. We need to show solidarity with our brothers.'

I could sense a few people nodding and agreeing with me and I got carried away into a rhetorical flourish. Subconsciously channelling Wodehouse, I added, 'It's true that DATA never stood behind us when we went on strike, but in the scheme of things . . . it matters not a jot!'

Not a jot. Who the fuck in Glasgow says 'not a jot'? Every head in the meeting turned towards me and I sensed an invisible thought bubble over each of them – *what the fuck was that?* And then the whole yard pissed themselves laughing at me. I couldn't say I blamed them.

There again, not many of the workers shared my developing interest in politics and world affairs. This became very clear at the end of October 1962 as the Cuban Missile Crisis looked to be nearing a terrible and possibly apocalyptic climax. America and the Soviet Union had ballistic missiles pointing at each other and looked set to use them, triggering a nuclear Armageddon and the end of the world as we knew it. On the morning of 27 October, the newspapers were reporting that they would most likely fire them at each other at 3 p.m.

My head was all over the place. I was expecting the planet to fall apart at three o'clock but it never happened, and when I went to the main shed to look at the big clock in there and saw that it was half past three, I figured that maybe we weren't going to be blown to smithereens after all.

When the work hooter went that day, I ran straight over to the *Glasgow Evening Times* seller outside the yard to get the latest on the complex international negotiations that had just saved the world. A load of other workers bought papers as well so I figured they were doing the same . . . until they all turned straight to the sports pages to see who was in the Celtic and Rangers teams that weekend.

The following year my apprenticeship came to an end. By then the music bug had got me; I had started playing wee gigs in Glasgow folk clubs and I knew I didn't want to go through life as a welder, but even so it felt important to me to finish my apprenticeship and get my papers.

By now everybody in the yard knew that I was playing little gigs on my banjo and wanted to leave to try to be a musician. In fact, that had become my nickname: Banjo Man. 'Oh, here he comes,' they'd say as they sat at tea break, and all started singing George Formby: *'Plonk plonk plonk, plonk plonk plonk plonk, when I'm cleaning windows!'* I tried pointing out that Formby played a ukulele, not a banjo, but they cared not a jot.

I spent a while hesitating about giving in my notice at Stephen's until Willie McInnes put the fear of God into me. One day when we were chatting, Bugsy asked me when I was going to quit the yard.

'I think in six months, after the Glasgow fair,' I told him.

'Och, you'll no do it,' he told me.

'What do you mean?'

'If you're putting it off now, you'll put it off again. Those six months will pass and then you'll say you're leaving six months after that. Then you'll do it again.'

Bugsy looked at me as I took his words in. 'Believe me, there's nothing worse than being an old man, still in here, thinking about what you could have done if you had got out when you were young,' he said, with feeling.

Fuck! I figured I had better quit there and then! It took me about two weeks to get my shit together and then I was out of Stephen's. I didn't have a big leaving do: I slid out quietly, just like I had when I left school.

My life changed a lot very quickly after that and so did I. I was away around Scotland doing one-night-stand gigs all the time and I began looking and dressing very different. After five years of welder's chaps and leather jackets, it was time to be somewhat more exotic.

I didn't keep in touch with the shipyard workers all that much. When I went back a couple of times to have a pint with the guys in the pub by the yard, I had an earring, was wearing court jester trousers and was festooned with beads. Naturally, they took the piss mercilessly. I would have hated it if they hadn't.

But I got involved with the shipyards again at the end of the decade. In 1968, the five major yards on the Clyde, including Stephen's, amalgamated and became Upper Clyde Shipbuilders. The general idea was for them to become more competitive on the world stage and enjoy economies of scale.

It didn't work. Upper Clyde Shipbuilders was making a loss, and in 1971 Edward Heath's Tory government declared that they would not subsidise any more 'lame duck' industries, as they charmingly called them. They refused to give UCS a loan and it went into liquidation, even though it had a full order book and was on target to make a profit the following year.

One of the yards, Denny's of Dumbarton, responded by selling off all their cranes and shipbuilding equipment to South Korea and to Australia, where the governments were still supporting industry. I seem to remember that Denny's went into pet food instead. There was no money, and Upper Clyde Shipbuilders began laying off the workers.

That was when the battle started. The Clyde yards had some brilliant union leaders then, and the best of all was Jimmy Reid. Jimmy was an extraordinary man. He was a proper socialist, self-educated but very well read, and he kind of made being a communist acceptable. I loved him to bits.

Jimmy was a real leader. He always put his case incredibly clearly and well and he instilled a sense of pride and nobility in the men. He made them feel proud of what they were, of being ship-yard workers and tradesmen, and got them to believe in themselves.

He was a fantastic speaker. It was a delight to hear him speak. He could sometimes get a wee bit carried away by his own rhetoric and the sound of his own voice. He'd make pronouncements at meetings like, 'The workers of Britain are getting off their knees and asserting their dignity!' Or he could get very index finger-y, pointing at the crowd to make his point as he testified: 'I will tell you once! I will tell you twice! I will tell you three times!' But even then, he carried them with him. He believed in them and they believed in him.

When Upper Clyde Shipbuilders began making workers redundant, Jimmy came up with a brilliant plan. The obvious thing would have been to go out on strike. Instead, Jimmy told the laid-off men to ignore their redundancy notices, come into work as usual and carry on building the ships – after all, there were plenty of orders! The other workers clubbed together to pay their sacked colleagues' wages.

This 'work-in' was a stroke of fucking genius. It totally threw the bosses and the government. Their whole thing was to say, 'The workers are work-shy and the trade unions are going against us and ruining things,' but here were the men filing in to work even after they'd been let go! It utterly confounded the Tories.

Jimmy organised this work-in and he was big on getting everything right. He knew they only had one chance. He told the tradesmen to work their hardest, do no damage to the yard and not spoil things by getting pissed: 'Nae bevvying', as he used to put it.

I was a few years out of the shipyards by then but I went to the

I used to think the Royal Family were a complete load of nonsense, until they started giving me things

Post-war Glasgow:
life in black and white

Just twenty miles out of Glasgow, the wonderful wilderness begins

A smile on the face of
an unhappy wee boy

One reason I was unhappy.
Let's call it tawse and effect

Drumchapel. No shops, cafés
or schools, but a remarkable
aerial display of shoes

In my Celtic seat for life, with Rod Stewart

Back in Drumchapel, with a milk float: I wouldnae jump on and off quite as quickly now

Rangers legend Willie Waddell: should I piss in his milk?

Jock Stein skinning Rangers' Derek Grierson; I'll never forget the crowds at Parkhead

A family gathering in
Stewartville Street.
That's me at the back
making my uncle laugh

The Sarrie Heid: mind the
flying scrumpy!

Everything about
Glasgow has changed
... except for the Sarrie

Barras Market:
where a Partick youth
became a cowboy

It always felt like the city's caurs were pals of ours

Somewhere in there, my washer is holding the *QE2* together

The Clyde shipyards were the beating heart of Glasgow

Jimmy Reid led a
revolution on the Clyde

19 August 2010: with
Sir Alex Ferguson at
Jimmy Reid's funeral

Listening hard at
an Upper Clyde
Shipbuilders meeting.
Original Humblebum
Tam Harvey is to my left

Voicing the yearning in every man: Hank Williams

Hank spoke to me then and he speaks to me now

Pete Seeger on the banjo: a sound too beautiful for words

Me on the banjo, also making a sound

There's never been another band like the Humblebums. Thank fuck

demonstrations to hear Jimmy speak and to show support and to get behind the tradesmen. The whole of Glasgow rallied behind the dock workers. They knew that the entire city was with them.

One day we all marched with the workers down to Glasgow Green. There must have been 80,000 people. Anthony Wedgwood Benn was the main speaker, and I took my banjo and played a few wee songs. It was a wonderful day and I was proud to be part of it. I felt like it was bigger than all of us, that we were making history . . . and that we were going to win.

Jimmy Reid actually went on *Parkinson* on the BBC before I did, arguing the workers' cause. He had a row with Kenneth Williams. On one famous occasion, Jimmy and I were on the show together. The other guest was a Hollywood legend, Lauren Bacall. I'm sorry to report she wasnae as well informed on the ups and downs of the Scottish shipbuilding industry as me and Jimmy.

Edward Heath came up to Glasgow and got booed but he kind of came around to the workers' side. He recognised their decency and the dignity of the working man, and he restructured the yards and gave them some government support. Old Ted even became quite liked on the Clyde.

The workers *did* win, in a way. Jimmy Reid's work-in earned the yards another two or three years from when they were first going to be closed down. But, even so, the tide was going against them and I guess in some ways they were only postponing the inevitable.

As the companies withdrew money from the shipyards, things got horribly grim. There were huge numbers of redundancies and there was just no way to re-employ those workers. And when Margaret Thatcher got in, things got even harder on the Clyde. Yet I'll never forget the nobility of those workers going into the yards even after they had been laid off. I've always been a union man, I still am, and I was so proud of them. I totally identified with them and what they were going through. I would march with them again tomorrow, if it all happened again.

It's still a puzzle to me, though: where did all those thousands of men *go*? All those men who worked in the docks, all the stevedores and dockers, all the riveters and the hole-borers from the shipyards, the platers and welders and caulkers, what happened to them? They weren't replaced by any other industry, so how did society soak them all up? Did they just get by on pensions? It baffles me.

When they got let go, they were hurt but defiant. They would say, 'If I have to, I'll go and sing around the back of the tenements!' Because you used to get these really broke guys in Glasgow in those days – winos, really – who would sing 'The Old Rugged Cross' behind the flats, and people would throw them a sandwich wrapped in paper, or a penny, out of the window. Actually, some of the singing winos were so fucking awful that people would throw them a penny to get rid of them. Or they'd play a wee trick, and heat a penny on the gas with pliers, then throw it out to them:

'Aye, thanks very much! Ouch! Ye bastard, you!'

I got very close to Jimmy Reid and he used to come out to my house for dinner. After he was on *Parkinson* he became even more of a Scottish legend. He ended up working for the papers, and he lost a bit of his shine when he wrote for the *Sun*, which was a shame, but he was a true hero.

I stayed in touch with Jimmy right until his death in 2010. I spoke at his funeral with Sir Alex Ferguson and Alex Salmond, the guy from the SNP. As we went along in the funeral car, all the men in the streets took their bonnets off, stood to attention and saluted the car. It was a great thing to see. He led a revolution on the Clyde and they loved him for it.

The shipyards gave Glasgow the dignity of labour for generations. People need to be employed. They need to do something with their hands and be occupied. It's when the employment goes down-hill that troubles in society start to rise. I think even a homeless guy, a bum at the bottom of the ladder, can stay sane if he has a way of getting through the day. If he can manage to beg enough money to get him through the night, he sleeps well, because it's been a successful day for him.

The Clyde shipyards gave thousands of men a purpose and an identity, and they did the same thing for Glasgow. We built the best ships in the world: the *Queen Mary*, the *Queen Elizabeth*, the *QE2*. We could say: 'That's ours: that's what we do.'

A while ago I went with Pamela to see the *Queen Mary*, which is docked in California now. We were in the ballroom on the ship just looking at the marquetry on the walls, which is magnificent work. I said to her, 'That was made by wee men in bonnets and overalls.' They just did it and sent it out to the world.

I did my years in the shipyards and they made me. They made me what I am, and the man that I am. I think back on them with great fondness and affection, and with love. But by my twenties I *could* tack the high road, right out of there, and that was what I did.

I wasn't that wee yodelly-voiced boy any more. I didn't know quite what I *was* yet, but I knew I was hairy and bearded and the world was there for the taking. All sorts of things were opening up, people were falling out with religion and saying, 'I'm not into money, man!' and it made me think, yes, *that's* the kind of world I want to live in.

When I quit the yard to play music and try my hand at entertainment I gave myself three months. And that was fifty years ago.

'*It Gets Us Alive Again . . .*'
A Conversation on Retirement

When I worked in the shipyard, men who retired would be given what was called 'a wallet of notes'. A foolscap sheet would come around the yard, saying 'Willy Johnson is retiring after thirty-five years', and we would all chip in a few pennies to his collection. On his final Friday afternoon, we would file down to the paint shop to stand around the guy, the poor victim, under a little Perspex awning, and a manager would make a wee speech. He'd say, 'Well, Willy, I suppose you'll be going to potter around in your garden now!' and we would all laugh, because we'd know Willy lived in a high-rise in the Gorbals. Then they would present him with his wallet of notes – a cheap wallet containing the money we had collected for him.

The guy who was retiring would be sent on his way, rejoicing. The next week he would show up on the Monday in the pub where we went for lunch, and maybe a few more days that week. That would go on for a month or two, and then he would just come down once a week or so, then maybe just once a month. His visits would fall away completely . . . and then we would hear that he was dead. A shipyard worker usually lasted eighteen months after he retired before he died. When he lost the job he also lost the sense of having a purpose to his life. It was a tragedy and, even as a young man of sixteen, I noticed it happening and realised that once a man's working life is over, he is in a very tender state and needs to be well treated and looked after.

A guy who retires from a job like that can get very lonely. He misses what he is used to – being around other men every day. Men like the company of men. It's not just to talk about women and sex and breasts. They like to talk about football, and politics, and life in general, and it's very beneficial for them to get together and do this. They also like to make things with their hands the way that they did when they were still part of industry. Nowadays they can do this in retirement thanks to the Scottish Men's Sheds Association, a fine organisation that brings men together in sheds and similar spaces during the week to chat, make weird and wonderful things, feel useful . . . and most likely add a few more years on to their lives.

The Men's Shed in Dalbeattie, near Dumfries in the Borders, won Best Men's Shed in Britain in 2017 and when you get inside its doors you can see why: it's a lovely, peculiar wee netherworld of squirrel dispatchers, World War I tanks, banter and male camaraderie. I met Dalbeattie shed secretary Geoff Allison, his mate Robin Gilchrist and some great, funny guys who, instead of sitting at home bored, lonely and twiddling their thumbs, are doing brilliant things for their local community . . . and for each other.

Geoff: Welcome to Dalbeattie Men's Shed, Billy.
Me: Thank you. So, how did this shed start off?
Geoff: A friend of ours, Brian Atwell, first had the idea.

Robin: There were about five of us. We looked for premises, that was the hard bit. Then a local businessman, Alan Mazza, who owns this space we're in here in Castle Works, offered to let us use it free of charge.

Geoff: Alan is very generous. We couldn't do this without him.

Me: How many members do you have?

Geoff: We have more than fifty signed up, and forty regulars. We meet two mornings per week and normally have about twenty people here at a time. Our average age is sixty-nine. Nearly all of us are retired and this gives us a task, it . . . *gets us alive again.*

Me: Aye. That's very, very important. Too many people retire and are just left to their own devices.

Geoff: Yes. The transition from work to retirement is hard and they can become reclusive. This gets them back among men.

Me: So, what kind of things do you make in here?

Jake: I'm making a dispatcher, Billy.

Me: Oh aye? Is Dalbeattie a bit of a roughhouse, that you're needing dispatchers?

Jake: No, this is for another cause – for trapping grey squirrels. We still have red squirrels up here and the grey squirrels have a pox, a disease, that carries over to the reds and kills them. The Americans introduced grey squirrels to this country. They are a foreign body.

Me: They introduced them for hunting, didn't they?

Jake: Aye. The grey squirrels are good for eating, though. Come to our Shed barbecue one night, I'll give you a grey squirrel leg. It's got a nutty flavour, obviously.

Me: Are you taking the piss?

Jake: I'm not up to taking the piss out of ye! It's true, barbecued grey squirrels are tasty.

Me: So, you just sneak up behind them with your dispatcher?

Jake: We have a squirrel trap that we check every day. We let the red squirrels go and dispatch the grey ones.

Me: And what is happening over here?

Geoff: Scotty is building a tank.

Scotty: Aye, it's a World War I tank. It's about half-scale. A normal tank is eighteen feet long and this will be about eight feet.

Me: Tanks were first introduced in World War I, weren't they?

Scotty: Yes. The Navy built the first ones. They came up with the idea of having land tanks. Churchill was Lord of the Admiralty and he said, 'Good idea.'

Me: I heard a story about World War I tanks. They had a door in the side of them.

Scotty: Aye, that's right.

Me: Enemy soldiers found it really hard to kill the guys in the tanks until somebody discovered that if you fired shells at the door, they went 'Knock-knock-knock' and they opened it . . . So, when will you be finished with your task?

Scotty: Hopefully next month. When I've finished it's going to go around the local schools for the children to see, then go on display in the town.

Me: Amazing. Is this what you did when you were a boy?

Scotty: Aye, I used to make plastic model kits. But this is the biggest scale-up I've ever done.

Me: I used to make model kits and then set them on fire.

Scotty: That could happen to this one yet. It might get hit by a German shell.

Me: Christ, I hope not. And what's happening here?

Geoff: This is our bike corner. The local police give us bikes they find that don't get claimed. We fix them and send them back into the community.

Me: I used to love cycling. And what is this thing?

Geoff: This is something we restored from being a rusty piece of scrap. It's an 1870s wood mortise which was once bought by a local firm for sixteen guineas – sixteen pounds and sixteen shillings.

Me: For mortising tenon joints?

Geoff: Yes, a hand one. Nowadays they are all electric. This is going to go into a museum. And over here, Derek is making garden furniture.

Derek: Hello, Billy. I remember seeing you play the Drill Hall in Dumfries.

Me: Oh, aye? Was I any good?

Derek: You were. You came on the stage, looked up, and said, 'It's the first time I've ever played in an effing aircraft hangar.' It was the first time I ever heard anybody swear on stage!

Me: That was a long time ago!

Derek: *Aye, it wasnae yesterday!* They were the good old days, eh? The Chic Murray days?

Me: He's a hero of mine. Did you make this furniture, Derek?

Derek: No, I'm painting it. I worked as a painter for fifty years and now I come up here and I do it for nothing. I can't get enough of it.

Me: My God, you do such a range of stuff here! I remember when I was a boy, I used to love to talk to the old guys in the park. They would all be playing dominoes, and cutting tobacco with knives, wearing their 'Old Contemptibles' badges from World War I.* I really looked up to them. They'd have loved a place like this to come to. Now, what on earth is that?

Geoff: This is our 3D printer. We get commissions – right now we're making a prototype of a little robot with accessories that a guy wants to sell to kids. It's quite complicated. Tim here does all this stuff.

Me: It sounds like witchcraft to me.

Tim: It is, but it is the technology of tomorrow. 3D printing is very slow now but when they get it sorted so it works at high speed

---

* During the First World War, the Kaiser in Germany had described the British Army as 'a contemptible little army'. He didn't call them that after they kicked his arse. The old ex-Army guys were proud of what they'd done and got badges made calling themselves the 'Old Contemptibles'.

it will change everything. You need a spare part? It will print it for you on the spot.

Me: They're even making spare parts for humans now.

Tim: Yes, they are.

Me: It's sinful! I love what you are all doing here.

Geoff: You haven't seen anything yet. This is Dr Oliver.

Me: You're an actual doctor?

Dr Oliver: Yes, I'm a GP. I'm helping to build a cycle-car here.

Geoff: There's quite a story to this. A guy named Bill Skeoch began building these things in Dalbeattie in 1920. He had built a dozen and sold them when his workshop set on fire. He wasnae insured so that was the end of his business.

Me: Oh, no. Why is it called a cycle-car?

Geoff: Because it's made of bicycle parts and powered with a two-stroke motorcycle engine, all inside a wooden chassis. This one's wheel is from a Chinese rickshaw. Bill Skeoch's grandson recently found the old plans and bits and wanted to get the car built in his grandfather's memory. When we won Men's Shed of the Year he read in the paper about us and the work we do, and thought maybe we could build it.

Me: That's brilliant.

Geoff: Bill Skeoch's daughter is still alive. She's ninety-four, and her dearest remaining wish is to sit in a car like her dad made. We want to let her do that.

Me: That's wonderful. How's it coming on?

Geoff: It's slow. We're trying to raise funds to buy things like wheels and springs – the things we can't make.

Me: Who provides the money for all your equipment?

Geoff: Last year we earned 80 per cent of it ourselves. The other 20 per cent was grants from people like Aid Scotland. We get donations from members and from people who come in to buy things. We only charge them for materials but most people are generous and give a donation on top.

Me: Well, I hope you get the cycle-car together.

Geoff: We will. We guys are from the make-do-and-mend era, aren't we? Nowadays everything is throwaway but we used to be in hand-me-down clothes, putting patches everywhere, making do.

Geoff Allison shows me around Dalbeattie Men's Shed

· · · · · · · · ·

Me: Aye. So, what time do you all start in the morning?

Robin: I was here at eight o'clock today and there was already
        somebody in. But when we retired, *they took the time away.*
        We don't have to clock in any more, we just wander in when
        we're ready.

Geoff: Most of the guys who come to the Shed didn't know each other
        before it started. They were pretty isolated in the community.

Me: Behind every miserable old bugger there's a reason.

Geoff: Yes, and behind every miserable old bugger there's a reason
        we have members! A lot of Dalbeattie wives have told their
        retired husbands, 'Look, it's a Men's Shed, get down there!'

Robin: Our friend Giorgio's wife called me up and asked, 'Can he
        come down to the Men's Shed?' I said, 'Aye, of course.' She
        said, 'He's Italian, though.' I said, 'That's OK, but we wouldn't
        take any English.'

Geoff: Steady on, Robin!

Robin: Ah, I'm only joking!

I think Dalbeattie Men's Shed is kind of a miracle – as are all the others
like it dotted around Scotland. I wish the guys that I worked with in the
shipyards sixty years ago had had something like this to go to when
they retired because I think that they would have lived a lot longer. I wish
them all the luck in the world with their tanks and cycle-cars, and I may
even call in there again some time for a barbecued squirrel leg.

'WHAT THE FUCK ARE YE WEARING AN EARRING FOR?'

There was always music in the house when I was a kid. My father and my aunts had records of Mario Lanza singing 'O Sole Mio' and Italian ballads, and Kenneth McKellar doing Robert Burns songs like 'Ae Fond Kiss' and traditional Scottish songs. Then we had the good old singing priests: preachers like Canon Sydney MacEwan, singing 'Bring Flowers of the Rarest'. The priests were always tenors, for some reason. I actually quite liked all that stuff.

Yet my own first musical awakening came in the unlikely setting of a Girl Guides' dance when I was about fourteen. A girl called Angie Hanlon, who lived in the next street, had asked me to go with her. At first it was all Scottish reels but then suddenly, out of nowhere, one of the girls produced a record and put it on. It was 'Heartbreak Hotel' by Elvis Presley, and the way the song fired into life was incredible:

'Well, since my baby left me – da-da! Well, I found a
new place to dwell – da-da!'

It was like nothing I had ever heard before, and I knew instantly that *this was for us*. It wasn't music for our parents and the adults of the world. This was aimed at us, and it was great.

After that, I started spending my milk round and bookshop earnings on music. I started buying Elvis records, and Bill Haley, Little Richard, Fats Domino, Chuck Berry. Those American stars all seemed to come in one big wave.

I liked some of the British guys as well, like Cliff Richard, Adam Faith and Marty Wilde, but they seemed like second-rate Americans; like copies. At that point, the only British musicians who played guitars were jazz musicians so they would be playing jazz chords, whereas the Americans had this blues and country influence and guitars and harmonicas that lifted you off the floor.

Just as I was getting into rock and roll, an American rockabilly singer called Charlie Gracie came to Glasgow. He had a hit called 'Butterfly' and I went to see him at the Glasgow Empire. It was the first rock show I ever went to and I loved it. It was still the days of variety theatre with a rock and roll star at the end of the bill, so the first half of the evening was jugglers and the like, being given a hard time by highly impatient Charlie Gracie fans: 'Fucking get off!' Maybe that's why you rarely see jugglers supporting rock bands these days.

I also got well into skiffle and people like Lonnie Donegan.

When he started doing stuff like 'Don't You Rock Me Daddy-o', guitars suddenly appeared in shop windows everywhere. I think Lonnie Donegan must have sold more guitars than any other human being. I was really moved by skiffle, and people like him and Chas McDevitt, and I began to memorise the words of all the songs.

I would play my singles on the family Dansette at home and my father and my aunts quite liked them because they were tuneful. It wasn't a foreign noise to them. They would shake their heads and tell me to turn it down a bit but they liked it when I played songs like 'Blueberry Hill'. They didn't mind them co-existing alongside Mario Lanza and the singing priests.

When I had just started work in the shipyards, there was a record I loved called 'Donna' by Ritchie Valens: *'Oh, Donna, oh, Donna!'* One day I was talking about it at work to a guy called Harry Brown and telling him that I wished I had it. 'I've got a copy of it,' he told me. 'But it's a 78 rpm. Do you have a record player that can play 78s?'

'Aye!' I told him, eagerly.

The next day Harry brought 'Donna' into work for me in its sleeve. That night I carried it like treasure to the Clyde ferry for my daily ride home. On the ferry, I was crushed right up against all the other welders and riveters and caulkers, so I put Ritchie Valens under my jacket to try to protect him. The boat suddenly tilted and a guy right next to me fell against me. A truly horrible sound came from under my coat: 'CRRRAAAACK!'

'CRRRAAAACK!' is rarely a good fucking noise, and it's

particularly not when you are carrying a vinyl record. I felt it snap so I reached into my coat and took it out. Shit! I was so pissed off that I grabbed the two halves of the single and *skiffed* them, as we Scots say, meaning skimming flat stones over water. I skiffed the two halves of Ritchie Valens over the side of the ferry and off down the Clyde. That was the end of poor 'Donna'. She went to a watery grave.

I loved rock and roll but it turned out really to be a flirtation, or a temporary infatuation, for me. It wasn't until I heard country music that I fell head over heels in love. My epiphany began one Saturday when my father took me down to the Barras, the market-place in the middle of Glasgow. There was a record dealer there and my dad bought a record without hearing it. It was 'Dear Mary' by Slim Whitman, and he assumed that it must be a hymn to Mary, Mother of Jesus. We got it home, and it wasnae: it was something completely different. It was a love song:

> *I'm writing this letter, dear Mary, to let you know how I feel,*
> *'Cause I'm lonesome and so weary, I can hardly eat a meal . . .*

I loved it as soon as I heard it. I loved the music and I loved the guy's singing style: Slim Whitman used to *yodel* in the middle of a line. Now, yodelling has never been big in Glasgow and I'd never heard anything like it before but I spent that whole week playing the song over and over, singing and yodelling along to it. My father noticed me doing it – it was quite hard to miss, in our tiny flat – and the next weekend he took me back to the same dealer at the Barras.

'I bought a record off you last week, "Dear Mary",' he said to the guy. 'Do you have anything else like it?'

'I havenae any more Slim Whitman but I have got this other guy you might like,' the dealer said, and he put a record on. It was 'Long Gone Lonesome Blues' by Hank Williams, and the second that I heard it, my life changed.

If you want to learn about songwriting, listen to Hank Williams. You can do no better. There is this lonesomeness in his voice, a yearning that is in every man, and I am no exception. Listening to 'Long Gone Lonesome Blues' in the Barras that Saturday afternoon, a cowboy was born in Partick, Glasgow. And I've stayed a cowboy all these years.

There's something weird about Hank Williams and country music, and what men do with it. When you lose a woman, you should go home and play music to cheer yourself up, but we never do that. Instead we go home and play sad songs that make our wounds even deeper so we can wallow in them. Hank specialised in that and I've used him for that purpose so many times in my life. I still do today.

It wasn't just the music of 'Long Gone Lonesome Blues' that got me, though. The sleeve had a picture of a character that Hank Williams had invented called Luke the Drifter. Luke was always walking into the sunset, with a guitar over his shoulder, and from that moment, that was how I saw myself and my future: forever walking into the distance, having broken a few hearts, on to my next adventure. I swore to myself there and then that that was going to be my life – the open road, and the guitar (and maybe the yodelling). A life of one-night stands.

I must have been fucking mentally ill, thinking that way at fifteen, but the strange thing is that for years, as I travelled from town to town doing one-night-stand shows, I felt like I was Luke the Drifter. I wanted to be windswept and interesting and roam the land singing songs, and being a patter merchant, and telling stories, and meeting women. I wanted my life to be everything that it wasn't while I was living a life of misery in a tenement in Glasgow with an aunt slapping me around the head. I wanted that music, and I pushed towards the sound with all my might.

Hank Williams was always the man for me but I began buying country and western records by other singers as well, a perplexing number of whom also seemed to be called Hank, like Hank Thompson, and Hank Snow. Hank Snow sang songs that told stories, like 'Old Doc Brown', and they really spoke to me.

Unless you bought the records, it wasn't very easy to hear that music in Scotland in the Fifties. There was a TV music show called *The White Heather Club* that usually played the stuff that my father liked, like Kenneth McKellar, but now and then they would have a folk band on, such as the Joe Gordon Folk Four. I loved the sound of the acoustic guitars but I didn't even know then that that music was called folk: I used to think of it as 'campfire music' because that was where I imagined it being played.

There was another TV show called *Alex Awhile*, which was hosted by two middle-class brothers named Alex and Rory McEwen. They both played big Gibson guitars and sang folk songs, and they had had lessons from the great blues singer and guitarist the Reverend Gary Davis in New York, which I was hugely impressed by. Then one week they had a special guest who totally blew me away.

I didn't know too much about the soon-to-be-legendary American folk and protest singer Pete Seeger then, but when I saw him on *Alex Awhile* it was a bolt of lightning to me. I'd heard the banjo on record before but I'd never seen anybody play one, and Pete Seeger singing 'Sacco's Letter to his Son' on TV did things to me. The sound of the banjo just seemed too beautiful for words.

'*That's* the noise I want to make!' I told myself. 'I'm going to get one of them.'

No sooner had Pete Seeger appeared on the TV show than he did a gig in Glasgow. It changed my life just as hearing Hank Williams had done. He played an old fretless mountain banjo, which I thought was amazing, and he sang blues songs and work songs and funny songs. He talked about Woody Guthrie and he played his song 'This Land Is Your Land' and chopped a log in half with an axe as he did it. The log split in half on the last line of the song and brought the house down.

Pete sang Tom Paxton's 'Ramblin' Boy' and by the end of it I knew every single word. It was stunning. He also did Bob Dylan's 'A Hard Rain's A-Gonna Fall'. I wasn't sure about Dylan at that point. A friend had played me his first album but it was foreign to me and it hadn't really clicked. Pete Seeger singing 'Hard Rain' was my proper introduction to Dylan, and then I went away and tried harder with him, and I *got it*. And nowadays I am a Bob Dylan fanatic.

I wanted a banjo more than anything in the world, and a few weeks after seeing Pete Seeger I got one. I went back to the Barras Market and there it was, a well-worn old zither banjo, like they used to play in Edwardian times, just hanging up behind one of the stalls. It cost me £2.50, which was my shipyard wages for a week, but it felt worth every penny. I couldn't have felt more excited – but how was I going to learn to play the thing?

There used to be an information centre in George Square in the city centre, the sort of place people went to ask for directions or where to get a bus to Fort William. On a Saturday afternoon I went in there and hit the lady behind the desk with a somewhat different request: 'Excuse me, but is there anywhere I can learn to play the five-string banjo?' She looked a wee bit perplexed, wandered off to find out, and came back with an answer: 'Try the Glasgow Folk Centre. It's three blocks away from here.'

She told me the Folk Centre held banjo, guitar and mandolin classes on Saturday afternoons, and when I got there and scurried upstairs with my banjo, the lessons were in full swing. In fact, the man who ran the centre, Jim Moyes, was holding a guy out of the window, three stories up, and yelling at him: 'Fucking give it me now!' I had no idea what the fellow had done to deserve that.

What I noticed even more than the guy being dangled three floors over the street, though, was that there was a record playing, *Songs of the Famous Carter Family* by Lester Flatt and Earl Scruggs, which was Appalachian bluegrass mountain music of just the kind I was getting into. When Jim had put the guy down I asked him about lessons and he took me over to the banjo teacher.

This guy, who had clearly styled his image on Dylan, tuned my banjo for me and taught me a few basic chords from a Pete Seeger book, which I already had at home. He was about six pages ahead of me but I began practising like crazy every minute that I was not at work. As somebody who had always been a poor student, I was delighted to find I was good at the basics of banjo-playing, and within six weeks I was better than my teacher.

By now my family had moved back from Drumchapel into Glasgow. We had tired of having fuck-all to do and buying our groceries from little green vans, and Florence had managed to persuade my father and our aunts to put their small savings into buying a flat in a tenement in White Street in Partick. I was just relieved to get out of the Scottish Siberia.

I was just out of my teens now and I threw myself into Glasgow life. Most weekends you'd find me in Clyde Books in Argyle Street. It was the left-wing bookshop for socialists and anarchists. The guys in the shop would advise me what books were good to read.

It was great that they were so helpful, as at that stage, before Willy Adams had opened my eyes in the shipyard, I knew the square root of fuck-all about political literature.

Looking back, I'm not sure that I would say that I was a communist in the early Sixties but I was certainly heading in that direction. My trade union experiences on the Clyde were teaching me that I was definitely left-wing. I was learning the political ropes: I wasn't a racist and I was all for women's equality. I was well learned in my Lefty ways, and I still am.

Yet the real draw of Clyde Books for me was its music section. They had great folk and banjo records by people I'd never heard of before such as the Ian Campbell Folk Group doing songs like 'The Sun Is Burning'. The guy who ran the shop would recommend those to me, as well – he was good at spotting a rebel, and it was through him that I got a love of Irish rebel music. He would let me play things in the shop to see if I liked them before I bought them. I was spending a lot of my shipyard wages in Clyde Books and every penny was well spent. I used to buy singles by folk singers – God knows why they released singles, because there was fuck-all chance of them ever getting into the charts – and then I moved on to buying the LPs.

One day I was walking along Argyle Street and I saw a shop that sold old typewriters. It had some second-hand LPs on a shelf and when I looked through them, there were autographed albums by this great US bluegrass duo called the Stanley Brothers. It was a gold mine for me, and I bought them. I often wonder how they had ended up in a second-hand shop in Glasgow. Had they belonged to some old guy who had gone to see the Stanleys, but now he had died and his wife had sold his collection on? It was wonderful to find them. I taught myself to play 'Clinch Mountain Backstep' from listening to them.

Rockers regarded folk music as naff, as if you were a softy for liking it. There weren't many big gigs, either. A couple of times a Blues and Gospel Caravan tour came to Glasgow with US artists like the Reverend Gary Davis, Mississippi John Hurt, Muddy Waters and Big Mama Thornton. They were colossal, but so foreign to me and so far out of my league – how could I possibly ever learn something like that?

But I was getting the urge to play music live. In 1964, I heard about a club in Paisley called the Attic Folk Club and I started going down there. It was in a club for old RAF guys called the RAF Society. They would put on folk gigs on Sunday nights and the locals would get up and sing for their guests. There would be about a hundred people there and it was fucking excellent. The resident band was a group called the Tannahills, who were brilliant. Their singer, Danny Kyle, would have the crowd in stitches in between the songs. He would come out with these outrageous dirty jokes and tear the place up. I genuinely had no idea till then that people could get away with saying things like that on a stage.

I introduced myself to Danny in the club and told him I was learning the banjo but I wanted to play it really well. He took me over to the Tannahills' banjo player, Ron Duff, who said that he'd give me a few lessons. Ron also had a wee side-band outside of the Tannahills, so after teaching me for a little while, during which I got a lot better, he made me the band's banjo player so he could become their guitarist. This happened a lot in those early days. I would learn to play banjo with a proper musician and then they would stick me in their band as the banjo player so it would free them up to play the guitar or mandolin. It seemed everybody else wanted to move on up from the banjo, and I was a rarity, or possibly a fucking freak, in that the banjo was then the height of my musical ambition.

I bought a better banjo, a Windsor Monarch, and I paid my dues playing in the pubs and clubs of Glasgow. There was a real innocence to that Glasgow folk scene. It was great. People didn't know much about banjo playing or the autoharp or the Carter Family – we were all just learning from the records. It was just as new to the audience so nobody was judging you harshly. I loved the fact that when the audience clapped the artists, the artists would clap them back. That to-and-fro, that *sharing,* really appealed to me.

The people I was playing with were teaching me as we went along – amazing guys and great pickers like Les Brown. I was into everything about the scene: the playing, the instruments, the hair, the clothes. I met Clive Palmer and Robin Williamson, who were to go on to form the Incredible String Band. They could play Appalachian stuff and Edwardian banjo and I thought they were superheroes. Soon I really wanted to have my own group so I formed a wee band called the Skillet Lickers with two guys named Jim Carey and George

McGovern. They were both far better banjo players than me, but the usual thing happened: Jim wanted to play guitar and George wanted to be on the mandolin, so I got to be the banjo player.

I loved doing the Skillet Lickers and I also joined another band, called the Acme Brush Company. That was a great experience. We had a very informal set-up: anybody who was around when we played a gig and knew a few chords could join the Acme Brush Company. If you knew the words, you were the singer for the night. We would skedaddle happily from a blues song about heroin to 'Goodnight Irene'.

Playing gigs at nights before clocking in to Stephen's early the next day meant a few very bleary mornings in the shipyard having the piss taken out of me, but the Banjo Man just didn't care. I was utterly consumed by the folk scene and still wanting to learn from anybody I could. I met a guy named Jimmy Steel, a lovely folk singer, and he gave me a few banjo lessons. He must have thought I was doing OK, because he suggested I should play with him, and maybe even do one or two songs on my own, when he played the Attic Folk Club the next Sunday.

It was to be my first ever solo performance and, on the night, I was so nervous it was ridiculous. I got up with Jimmy at the start of the show and played banjo while he did a few songs like 'Kelly the Boy from Killane'. Then the moment came. Jimmy put his guitar down, told the audience, 'Well, Billy's gonna sing you a song now,' and left the stage.

I was up there on my own and I started getting weird flashbacks to being a wee boy and fainting in church during a service. It was the only time in my life that I could remember everything feeling quite so unreal, with everybody staring at me. I started singing a song called 'St Brendan's Fair Isle' by a guy called Jimmy Driftwood, who also wrote a famous folk song called 'The Battle of New Orleans'. 'St Brendan's Fair Isle' is about the saint sailing from Ireland to America in a leather boat. My rendition of it was going fine at first but then my nerves kicked in, my brain froze and I forgot the words. I suppose I could have just hummed or apologised and called Jimmy back to the stage . . . but, instead, I did something else.

'Well, I've forgotten the words here, but I'll tell you what happens in the song anyway,' I told the Attic Folk Club, continuing to strum my banjo as I spoke. 'The priest is in the leather boat, see, on his way to a new life in America. He sees an island on the way, moors his boat next to it and steps onto it, but as soon as he sets foot on the beach, the island ups and swims away, because . . . would you believe it? It's actually a whale . . .'

As I spoke I was expecting to hear a few boos for this hapless young banjo player who had forgotten his lyrics, but instead something weird happened. As I embroidered the story and chucked in a few jokes and daft comments, people were smiling, and then they began to laugh their heads off at what I was saying. They were on my side. When I finished they didn't just applaud, they gave me a loud cheer – 'Hooray!'

I could not have been more delighted. I absolutely loved it. *Oh, I want more of this!* I thought, just the same as I had when I was sitting in a puddle, aged seven, in the playground at St Peter's, or trying to make the other welders laugh over mugs of black tea in Stephen's. Trying to be a patter merchant.

One night in the Attic Folk Club I met a guitarist called Tam Harvey. Tam was from a similar working-class background to me and I loved the way that he played guitar. He had been a rocker, so he knew how to play up the neck of the guitar. We got chatting, started practising together and decided we would become a duo. One night we were at a party and somebody suggested we should be called the Stumblebums. 'Huh! Humblebums, more like!' somebody else said. I thought that was a brilliant name, so that was it: the Humblebums we were.

It was a joy being a Humblebum. Scotland was developing a healthy folk scene by then with clubs in Edinburgh, Dundee and Inverness and a lot of smaller towns as well. They were often run by the local universities, or else they would just be in an upstairs room in a pub. So the Humblebums set off on a succession of one-night-stand gigs up and down the land. Tam and I both penned songs. At first, I just used to write ballads about love. I've told people for years that they were shite, but I listened to some again not so long ago, and they weren't that bad. They were just *ordinary.**

---

* Oddly, over the years people have come to quite like my Humblebums stuff and recently, for the first time in decades, I've had the urge to write songs again. I might just buy myself a wee electronic keyboard and see what happens.

Tam was as hairy as me, with hair and ringlets down to his waist but a wee bit thin on top, and we looked quite the pair. I also started dressing very flamboyantly for shows. There was a reason for that – well, I mean in addition to the fact that I love loud clothes. I used to turn up for gigs in Levi's, looking like everybody else. The doorman would have no idea who I was and I'd have to explain: 'I'm Billy Connolly, I'm in the Humblebums.' Eventually I got tired of that and started buying wild clothes from boutiques. I'd turn up in psychedelic trousers with stars or rainbows on. The doormen fucking knew that I was in the band then!

The Humblebums roamed up and down the country playing our wee songs. I began to feel I really was living the life I wanted: being Luke the Drifter, always moving on. I discovered to my delight that even big hairy banjo players in rainbow trousers could get groupies. Going with loads of women had always been a big part of my adolescent fantasy of being a windswept and interesting rambling man and here I was, living the dream.

The groupie is a much unfairly derided creature. They were just girls who liked guys in bands and the ones I met were always nice people. One time, Tam and I were in Arbroath. We had just played a club and we heard that a local pub called the Windmill had a good folk night on a Sunday so we wandered down there and did a floor spot for nothing. The promoter gave us ten shillings and said, 'Aye, lads, you're great, could I book you for next week?' We said fine, and rather than go back to Glasgow for five days we stayed in Arbroath, chatting up the local women, getting off with them and staying with them.

Another night, in Edinburgh, I met a girl at a show and we went back to her place. It was full of hippies who were playing Grateful Dead records and had put a cylinder of paper on the record player with holes cut in it and a light bulb inside. The girl had a military sleeping bag for two, so she and I got into it and I fastened the top string nice and tight around us. At which point she puked all over me. That was the end of romance for that night.

Back in Glasgow, Tam and I wandered into the Scotia Bar in Sackwell Street one night. It was right next to the Scotia Theatre but that had burned down, so now the bar was kind of dead. A few guys from the fish market nearby would go in during the day but in the evenings, it was empty. So, the landlord didn't mind at all when we took in our guitars and banjos and started playing gigs there. Over the weeks, more people started coming in and the Scotia became a trendy place to be.

I was drinking there one night when a guy called Keith Darvill came over and introduced himself. He was a theatre director and said he had heard that I was a banjo player and he was looking for musicians for a play that he was directing at the Citizens Theatre in the Gorbals called *Clydeside*, about the socialist movement in Glasgow in the early twentieth century. He asked if I'd be willing to provide the music. 'Well, I'm not too bad,' I said, 'but my mate Tam is ten times better. I'll bring him with me.'

I'd never seen a play in my life before but Tam and I went down and pitched in. I played the banjo and autoharp, which I had recently picked up, and Tam was on guitar and mandolin. *Clydeside* was a great socialist drama and in the cast was Richard Wilson, who later went on to be Victor Meldrew in *One Foot in the Grave*. He was slightly older than me and more theatrical, so there was a bit of a distance between us at first, but we became friends and we have seen a lot of each other's shows in the half a century since then.

The rehearsals for *Clydeside* were during the daytime, when I was supposed to be welding, and this and my pep talk from Willie McInnes were what led me finally to give in my notice at Stephen's. It felt time to do it. The music side was starting to go well, interesting things were happening and, as Willie had said, what the fuck was I waiting for? So, the shipyard gates closed behind me for the last time. My sister, Florence, was really pleased I was trying to go professional as a musician but the rest of my family thought I was being stupid. My father and my aunts thought that it was misguided and foolish. My granny was the most horrified of all. 'What, ye are giving up welding to play the banj-o?' she asked me, incredulously, putting all the weight on the 'o'. 'Ye're giving up to play the banj-O?'

Aye, I was giving up welding to play the banj-O, and I was also looking more and more way out. By now my wild clothes weren't just restricted to gigs: I was wearing them as I went about my daily business around Glasgow. I also decided to get my ears pierced. A pal tried to do it with ice cubes and a needle. It hurt like fuck but it worked until the holes healed up, so I went to a shop called Robin Hood and they did it properly. Then I was meandering around the city in big hooped earrings. This was a somewhat unorthodox look for an ex-welder in Glasgow in the Sixties and it got its fair share of comments. I started getting hassled in the street every day, but I loved that. In a funny way, it made me feel special. Glaswegians are a uniquely direct species, and people would come marching up to me and get straight to the point:

'What the fuck are ye wearing an earring for?'

'Because it makes me attractive!' I would tell them. I got particularly relentless attention when I went to watch Celtic: 'Fuck me, man, will you look at the state of you!' But it was all quite nice-natured and nobody ever took a swing at me. It was fun.

Plus, of course, it was the Sixties. I had totally bought into the hippy dream of peace and love and not caring about money, *man*. I was a folk music guy but I also loved the Beatles and the Stones and to me it was all part of the same thing – rebellion, and changing the world, and not being part of the dreary old ways of doing things. The Sixties felt like a chance to *start again as a person*: like you weren't just a product of your parents or your religion or your schooling. It was up to you – you could be whatever you wanted to be.

I was rejecting the old conventional world of religion and work and being repressed, but I didn't feel angry or contemptuous about that world – I just felt, *things could be done better*. It was OK to tell people that you loved them. I told my father that I loved him, but he never said it back. I understood that completely: his generation *just didnae*. But the world was changing and, rambling around Glasgow in my loon pants and my Afghan coat, with my hair down my back, I felt as if I was in the vanguard of that change. It was a lovely feeling to have.

For a working-class lad from Glasgow with a childhood like mine, the Sixties were wonderful, a chance to redefine yourself and the world you were in, and I grabbed it with both hands. I knew that *this was our time*. I suppose, really, we hippies were all luvvies, but so fucking what? I would rather be a luvvy than be loveless. Nowadays, people like the *Daily Mail* blame the Sixties for the collapse of civilisation as they know it but frankly I think the Sixties didn't go far enough, or there wouldn't *be* a *Daily Mail*.

Of course, there were different kinds of hippies around. I was very working class and rock and roll and a lot of them were middle-class guys, in their corduroy jackets with a copy of Tolkien peeping out of the pocket. If I am honest, that lot used to bore me shitless. I didn't exactly feel part of their whole 'tune in, turn on, drop out' mentality – I was just doing my own thing, being Luke the Drifter. Dope was everywhere in the hippy and folk scenes, but it never did it for me. I would join in when the joints got passed around and it would be great for a minute or so but then it would have a horrible effect on my head. It would fog me up and last too long and I wouldn't be able to get it to go away. I used to be jealous of the guys who were just stoned and having a good time.

It wasn't all peace and love in Glasgow then, to say the least. One night I went to a pub called the Marland Bar, just along from the Folk Centre. As I went to open the glass-panelled door, a guy came through the panel head-first. He was hanging there then was pulled back inside before the door opened, and he was unceremoniously booted out: 'Get the fuck out of here!' There was broken glass everywhere. I went in anyway and saw Hamish Imlach, a folk singer I loved, happily playing his guitar by the fireside. Now *this* is my sort of pub, I thought.

Hamish was a brilliant guitarist but also very funny and it was almost intimidating – I used to think, *I'll never be as good as him.* Tam and I would also sometimes play live backing Matt McGinn. Matt had an amazing story. He was a Glaswegian who had left school at twelve and worked in a local factory before studying politics at Ruskin College, Oxford, like Willy Adams had wanted me to do. He became a teacher but he was also a folk singer and he won a song-writing competition in a newspaper called the *Reynold's News.* One of the judges of the competition was Pete Seeger's sister, Peggy Seeger, and she told Pete about him. Pete championed him and arranged for him to play Carnegie Hall in New York, where he met Bob Dylan.

Despite all that, though, Matt wasn't very musical. Tam was always great at finding the right key for a song, and he had to be when we played with Matt. Matt would just start singing without consulting us, and behind him I would be whispering to Tam, 'What is he doing *now*? Which fucking key is this?'

'Pull him into G,' Tam would say to me. 'Let's tow him into G.'

With the Humblebums, I was still bringing humour into the gigs. I wrote a song called 'Windy and Warm', which I'd introduce by saying, 'I'd like to dedicate this song to nervous flatulence.' There was sometimes an edge to my patter, as well. When we played Dunfermline, I dedicated a song to the poor people who seemed to end up in A&E after being nicked, taken down the local police station and 'falling down the stairs'. The song was the Crystals' 'Then He Kissed Me', but I'd sing, 'And then he kicked me'.

One night, the Humblebums did a charity gig at the Orange Hall in Paisley, and at the end of it a guy came up to introduce himself to me. His name was Gerry Rafferty and he was with a mate whose name was also Gerry. 'That was brilliant!' he told me. 'I loved it, you were very funny.'

'Thanks, I'm glad you liked it,' I told him.

'Do you want to come back to my place?' Gerry asked. 'I write songs as well . . .'

Oh Christ, here we go, I thought. I'd had this happen a few times before and had always ended up sitting enduring some guy strumming some dreary dirge about being dumped that inevitably rhymed 'rain' with 'window pane'. Not again . . .

'We're having a few beers as well,' Gerry added.

I was suddenly keener. 'Aye, OK then, let's go!'

We went back to Gerry's house and he played us a few of his songs and I thought he was kidding me on. I thought he was taking the piss. The songs were so sharp and sophisticated that they sounded like songs from the hit parade, and I thought that he must be copying them from some album that I didn't know.

'Are those *really* your songs?' I asked him.

'Aye.'

'Christ, you're fucking brilliant! Would you like to join the band?'

'Aye, I would like that.'

It was as natural as that: a quick chat at a gig, a couple of songs over a beer, and Gerry Rafferty was in the Humblebums. Of course, I had got rather carried away and not cleared this with Tam first, and now I had to talk him round to us becoming a three-piece. He wasn't as into Gerry's slick sound as me and didn't want the band to go in that musical direction. I talked him into it, though, and we did some gigs as a trio. Tam and Gerry rubbed along part of the time but there was a discomfort, an awkwardness, between them and it wasn't really ideal. The Humblebums didn't seem to work so well as a three-piece and I took a difficult decision after a particularly dodgy gig at the Kinema Ballroom in Dunfermline, where Tam had made a few mistakes. 'You're going to have to fire him,' Gerry told me. I hated the idea because Tam and I had had such good times and been through a lot, but in my heart, I knew that Gerry was right. It was a horrible conversation, and Tam took it badly, but now the Humblebums were a duo again.

Bringing Gerry in took the band up to another level. He was on a path to success, as he saw it, and dedicated to making it with his songs. He was very driven. 'We are worthwhile, we are good, we will be successful,' he would tell me. 'It's good material. It *has* to be successful if we do it right!' His attitude was a new thing for me and it affected me, in a good way. It still does. To this day I will think, *I'm good because I'm good.* It's a nice knowledge to have.

Gerry and I got on like a house on fire at the start. We had similar views on the world and although he was always serious on stage, Gerry had a great sense of humour and shared my love of practical jokes. One thing we both loved doing was scouring local newspapers while we were on the road to find ridiculous stories. I still remember reading about a guy somewhere in Scotland who worked in an abattoir, and in his passport had given his job description as 'killer'. He was most indignant at not being allowed into Spain for his summer holidays.

Now Gerry was in the Humblebums, I realised even more just what an amazing songwriter he was. We were both writing songs for the band but his were just so much better than mine. I was coming up with humorous little songs like 'Back to Dunoon', about a somewhat limited and parochial wee town whose seaside location had made it into a Scottish holiday resort:

> *Why don't they come back to Dunoon?*
> *This switched-on scene*
> *Has two pubs, three cafés and a fire machine*
> *And hills you can walk on while the rain rung doon*
> *A night life that stops in the afternoon . . .*
> *Why don't they come back to Dunoon?*

I also wrote a song about the home where I was born being knocked down. One night I had gone round to see a friend who lived in Dover Street. We had got mighty pissed and I had crashed out there for the night. The next morning, hungover and splashing my face in the kitchen sink, I glanced up and out of the window just in time to see No. 65 being demolished and collapsing into a mountain of rubble. Of course, being a daft wee hippy, I thought this must be significant. I wrote a song about seeing my tenement come down:

> Oh, I was born in Glasgow
> Near the centre of the town,
> I would take you there and show you
> But they pulled the building down.

It was fun but it wasn't in the same league as 'Her Father Didn't Like Me Anyway' and 'Shoeshine Boy' and the other stuff that Gerry was coming up with and so I stopped writing songs for a while because they were being so overshadowed by Gerry's material. I didn't mind too much because I was bringing something else to the party. My comedy routines between the songs were getting longer and more inventive.

I don't think that there has ever been another group like the Humblebums. We were the weirdest outfit. Gerry would sing these extraordinary songs, not just his own but brilliant versions of standards like 'Summertime'. People were just flabbergasted by how good he was. I would step in and tell a story and have them roaring with laughter, then he would sing another song. We weren't like Cannon and Ball, with a straight man and a funny man: we were an inventive funny guy and a very inventive singer/songwriter. I deeply respected his music and Gerry deeply respected my funny.

We toured a lot, playing bigger and bigger theatres, and we met some amazing people on the road. We knew Mike Harding, and Jasper Carrott, and it seemed to me like they were doing the same thing as me: playing folk and talking about their lives and trying to be funny with it. I met Bert Jansch, an amazing folk guitarist who made a totally original noise. He told me once that Davey Graham had recommended he hear the wonderful music in Morocco. Bert used to always wear a duffle coat, and he went off to Morocco to hear the music, still wearing it. Bert is gone now, but every time I think of him, I get this mental image of him walking across a desert, in his duffle coat, with a guitar case.

The Humblebums often ventured down to England and one night we played near London, at the Beckenham Arts Lab at the Three Tuns pub in Kent, and I saw a young David Bowie. He wasn't known then but he had very long peek-a-boo hair and he looked like a female film star. I couldn't believe my eyes when he came out to sing. He had a cotton headscarf around his head, so you couldn't see his face, and he sang through the cloth. It was really dramatic, and I thought, *God, I'm going to see a lot more of this guy.*

I always loved being on the road, but back in Glasgow my life took a major turn as the Sixties ended. I had met a lovely girl, Iris Pressagh, who played the autoharp in folk clubs, and started dating her, and after a few months she told me she was pregnant. I might have been a long-haired, anti-establishment, beatnik drifter at the time, but even so I had absolutely no doubt about the right thing to do.

I had moved out of my family home by now and was staying with Danny Kyle at the time. I went through to see him with a question:

'Eh, Danny, how do you get married? What do you do?'

'It costs seven and six,' he told me (and that would be a mighty 37½p in today's money). 'You go to Martha Street and give them the money. They post the banns then you just turn up on the day. Easy.'

Easy it was. Gerry was my best man at the wedding and we even played a Humblebums gig that night. A few months later, my son, Jamie, was born, and Iris and I moved with him into a poky Glasgow tenement flat. Iris was an interior designer, and as a statement of our irrevocably bohemian natures, we sawed all the legs off our dining chairs and painted the place purple. Cosmic!

With my penchant for unconventional living, wandering the land and one-night stands, you might have thought settling down to domestic life would strike me with absolute horror, but in fact the opposite happened. Life with Iris was good and I loved being a dad. I was a hippy, and I saw the best in everything: I just thought that I had now become windswept and even *more* interesting.

Home life was good but the Humblebums had hit a rocky

patch. After Gerry and I had been together for two or three years, tensions began to creep in. There were clues when we went into the studio to make our albums. Tam and I had made a little record in the band's early days and we had a good laugh in the studio, but it was different with Gerry. He was a perfectionist and he wanted really high production values, like the Beatles or Harry Nilsson. We would do take after take after take, and it would bore me shitless.

Gerry was getting restless at my lack of musicianship. He got the urge to be surrounded by more sophisticated musicians and so our record label hired some session men to play in the studio with us. Also, I was doing really well with my storytelling on stage, but I was getting the vibe that Gerry was getting fed up with me going on for so long. I would glance over and see him sitting on his stool with his guitar, watching me, looking impatient at having to wait for me to finish my story before he could sing another song.

These tensions weren't unique to us, of course. They have happened to every band, from the Rolling Stones to Simon & Garfunkel. This strain comes between the members, threatening their friendship, and they start thinking they should be getting further ahead, and the other guy is holding them back. It's the classic thing that ends up in big bands arriving at venues in separate limousines, having separate dressing rooms and throwing hissy fits:

'He's got more mirrors in his room than me!'
'He's got a wash basin, and I haven't!'

Gerry and I were nowhere near that level and things never got as bad as that, but by 1971 it felt like things were running down. It all came to a head at Queen Street station in Glasgow. We were waiting to get a train out to Dundee and Fife to play some east coast gigs and we appeared to be having major trouble talking to, or even looking at, each other.

'This is daft, Gerry,' I said to him. 'I think we've come to the end of it, don't you? I think we should do this last Scottish tour and save the money from it, and then split. You go your way and I can go mine. We've taken it as far as it can go.'

'Aye, I agree,' said Gerry. He looked relieved that I had said it. Then the next morning he took me to one side. 'Listen, Billy, I've been thinking,' he said. 'I think we've taken this as far as it can go and we should split.' *Well*, I thought, *I wonder what gave you that fucking idea?*

We split perfectly amicably, as the friends that we still were, and Gerry went off to form Stealers Wheel and do very well for himself. I shall always think fondly of my wonderful time in the Humblebums but by the end of the group he and I had grown up and apart and were looking for different things from music and from life. In fact, as I always tell people who ask me why we split up: it was the Big Yin and the Big Yang.

After our last tour ended, I did the thing that every dippy old hippy does and went away to get my head together. I had some friends up in Glencoe. They had a caravan which they lent to me while I pondered the big question: what was I going to do next?

People knew that Gerry was the main songwriting talent in the Humblebums and I think that many assumed that after we split, he would go on to fame and fortune while I sank back into obscurity. I couldn't allow this to happen – I had a family, for one thing – so I started playing solo gigs in smaller venues than the ones we had played as the Humblebums. Now Gerry had gone, the balance of my shows shifted and they were probably three-quarters comedy and one-quarter humorous songs. I was just ticking over, I suppose . . . and then Jesus came to save me and show me the light.

Jesus from Gallowgate.

'Skinny Malinky Farted...'
A Conversation on Fine Art

When I was in my mid-teens, my sister Florence escaped our aunts and our house of misery and went off to study at the teacher training college at Notre Dame in central Glasgow. She loved it there, which made me very happy, and I always enjoyed going to visit her on campus on Sundays.

Florence would sometimes take me to the Kelvingrove Art Gallery and it made a huge impression on me. Some of the art there was just amazing. I was completely blown away by Salvador Dalí's *Christ of Saint John of the Cross*, which I thought was the greatest painting I had ever seen. Sixty years on, I might still think that.

I also loved the Kelvingrove because it had these fantastic slippery marble floors and I could take my shoes off and run and slide at great speed between its many artistic masterpieces. It's very odd the gallery staff never seemed to object to me doing that. I've no idea why.

Those teenage trips sparked in me an appreciation of great art to rival my love for literature. I've even got to know one or two major Scottish artists – not least the deeply estimable John Byrne.

I first met John in 1968, through Gerry Rafferty. He designed album sleeves for the Humblebums and later for me, and he designed my famous bananas boots that I used to wear on stage in my early comedy years. He's always made me laugh a lot. When I phoned John, I'd usually lie on the floor before I made the call because I knew that was where I was going to end up, so I figured I might as well start there.

But John's done a wee bit more than make me howl with laughter. He's a formidable guy. He made it out of the schemes of Paisley to become a fantastic playwright about Scottish working-class life, including 1978's brilliant *The Slab Boys Trilogy*, and TV series like *Tutti Frutti*. He is also an acclaimed artist, and the subjects of his many paintings in Scotland's National Portrait Gallery in Edinburgh include himself, his former partner Tilda Swinton, Robbie Coltrane . . . and me.

My lifelong friend, the deeply estimable John Byrne

John used to paint portraits of me and then he'd add these amazing clothes that I loved but wasn't actually wearing at the time – in fact, I'd never seen any of them in my life. And last year he did a portrait of me as one of three murals that went up on walls around Glasgow to mark the august occasion of my seventy-fifth birthday.

I've known John Byrne for exactly a million years. Recently, he and I met up and ambled around the Portrait Gallery with all the alacrity that you would expect of two friends who are 153 years old between us. We didn't take our shoes off and slide on the floor but, reading these edited highlights of our hugely informed art criticism, you may wonder if that was our only concession to the maturity you'd expect of two gentlemen of our remarkable vintage.

Indeed, it may help if you read the following dialogue with a mental image of Waldorf and Statler from *The Muppet Show* . . .

John: Eh, who's this guy here? Ah, James V!

Me: Extraordinary outfits.

John: Aye, I know. Not even wearing a tie. What's this guy pointing at?

Me: I don't know. It looks like a stick of cinnamon he's got. Look, here's Margaret Tudor.

John: Ah. Very lovely.

Me: She was known as Two-Frames Tudor.

John: That's right. She's pale. Pale is what I like.

Me: Here's Mary, Queen of Scots.

John: Ah, God, so it is, yes.

Me: 'Artist unknown'. It wasn't you, was it?

John: No. I painted her later, in 1987. That must've been when she was turned in. She has nice red hair and a beautiful frame.

Me:	She had a wee dog under her dress. When she was executed the wee dog ran out from under her dress.
John:	Aye. That is an interesting fact. What happened to it?
Me:	I don't know. I think we beheaded the dog as well.
John:	Who is this?
Me:	[*reads*] George, Lord Seton, Master of the Household of Mary, Queen of Scots. Attributed to Adrian Vanson. It's pretty good, isn't it?
John:	Aye, it's brilliant. It's beautiful. He's got a slight cleft in his chin. A good nose. Very thin lips.
Me:	Snake lips . . . Look, here's Henry Stuart, Lord Darnley.
John:	Aye.
Me:	He was the lover of Mary, Queen of Scots, wasn't he?
John:	Was he? He just looks like a boy.
Me:	He had syphilis, as well.
John:	No! At that age?
Me:	Well, I don't know if he had it there. It's good, that painting, isn't it? The black on the black background.

Henry Stuart, Lord Darnley
by Hans Eworth

John:	It's very beautiful, very subtle. Who painted it?
Me:	Hans Eworth.

John: Oh God, yes! Aye!

Me: Have you heard of him?

John: No.

Me: He was very good, Hans, for his time. He was known as
Black-on-Black Hans. Painter Black Hans. Makes me happy.
And there's James VI. He was brought up a Protestant.

John: That's true, yes. He's very young there . . . Who's this guy?

Me: George Buchanan. A classical scholar and historian.

John: Oh. He's going to let go of that book.

Me: He looks a bit of a twister.

John: Yes.

Me: He was one of Mary, Queen of Scots' courtiers. [reads] He
turned against her following the murder of her husband, Lord
Darnley. He accused Mary of being unfit to rule and his vicious
accusations helped destroy her reputation.

John: Oh, bugger!

Me: He was the tutor to that wee boy, James VI. I don't like the
look of him, Buchanan.

John: No, nor me. Bad-looking bugger . . . Who's this picture?

Me: I think it's you, John.

John: I think it might be.

Me: [reads] James Douglas, 4th Earl of Morton. One of the last
Protestant lords to destabilise the reign of Mary, Queen of
Scots. She wasn't short of enemies. His hands are a bit sus,
aren't they?

John: Aye, big paws. And another ginger.

Me: Yes, there's plenty of gingers.

John: I don't get the thing about ginger hair. I love ginger hair.

Me: I like it, too. I saw a drag guy on TV talking about ginger hair.
        He said that ginger pubic hair looks like a nest of baby mice.

John: So many Scottish and Irish people are ginger. Look, here it is
        on another one.

Me: Lady Agnes Douglas, Countess of Argyll. It's wonderful, that
        painting of the lace, isn't it?

John: Yes, that would be starch with sugar . . . Now, this one here – I
        recognise that face.

Me: I think I know him. Let me see . . . Tom Derry, Anne of
        Denmark's fool of a jester.

John: Aye, he does have a comical face.

Me: He reminds me of somebody from the Labour government . . .
        Oh, this one is brilliant!

John: This is Esther Inglis. I love her hat.

Me: Yes, this is my favourite so far. I wonder if people ever insisted
        they were made better-looking than they are? You know, 'Give
        me a better nose'? 'Don't give me so much forehead'?

John: It's strangely under-flattering. What's that in her hand?

Me: I was going to say it is a watch, but they didn't have watches
        then, did they?

John: Maybe they carried mini-sundials round with them. What
        about this picture here? What kind of dog is that?

Me: I don't know.

John: It's just half a dog.

Me: Aye, she was famous for having half a dog.

John: Oh God, there's a Campbell over there.

Me: That's a *sleekit*-looking face if ever I saw one.

John: He couldn't even smile for his own portrait.

Me: He's definitely spotted boys stealing apples off his tree. What a horrible-looking guy.

John: Aye. Who is he?

Me: The Marquess of Argyll. Archibald Campbell.

John: Ah, the Campbells are coming!

Me: [*reads*] Chief of the Clan Campbell and political leader of the Covenanters. His father described him as 'a man of craft and falsehood'.

John: Well, I don't doubt that.

Me: Definitely looks like a liar to me.

John: Aye, and his eyes do follow you around the room.

Me: The left one certainly does.

John: Maybe he had an implant.

Me: Mind you, we'll say anything about Campbells.

John: I know!

Me: They don't get good PR.

John: Oh my God, look at this one!

Me: Oh my God, he's been beheaded! Who is it?

John: Charles I. This is the execution of Charles I.

Me: Oh, is that the guy who was beheaded in Parliament?

John: It drew a big crowd. His execution was a great draw. Good Lord, there's the head!

Me: Well, that's hellish, isn't it? . . . Oh, this is better! That's brilliant. It's Lord Duffus.

John: His mother always said he was a good eater, as you can tell.

Me: He never left a thing on his plate, that boy.

John: Lord, what a great kilt, as well!

Me: It's a splendid kilt, isn't it?

John: Aye. It's a wee bit on the short side, but the Scottish Royals liked a mini-kilt.

Me: I've never seen a kilt with pockets like that.

John: Nor have I. It's to keep all his coins for the bus.

Me: Duffus has become a bad word. A doofus is an idiot in America . . . Now this is a famous one, isn't it?

John: I think it is. Charles Edward Stuart.

Me: Prince Charles Edward Stuart. Bonnie Prince Charlie.

John: He was invited to be the king of America and turned it down.

Me: He was invited . . . what?

John: To be the king of America.

Me: Are you kidding me on?

John: No, no, it's a fact. I just heard it recently. Think how much that would have changed history. King Charles Edward Stuart of the USA.

Me: It's a good picture, isn't it? He was an Italian.

John: Who, the guy who painted it?

Me: No – Bonnie Prince Charlie.

John: Italian?

Me: Aye, he was born in Italy and his mother was Polish.

John: Oh. That's maybe why he was invited to be the king

of America.

Me: Aye.

John: Was he in the Mafia?

Me: It was the only time Scotland was ruled by a gay Italian dwarf.

John: Is that right?

Me: He lived in a shortbread tin in the Highlands . . . Ah, here is

Alexander Murray of Elibank.

John: Oh, there we are.

Me: He was hung, drawn and quartered.

John: Really? Good Lord!

Me: Oh, hang on. No, he wasn't.

John: Thank God.

Me: It was Archibald Cameron of Lochiel who was captured in

the Highlands.

John: Right.

Me: *He* was hung, drawn and quartered.

John: Who is that picture again? Glenn Campbell?

Me: No, that is Alexander Murray.

John: So he's not the guy who was hung, drawn and quartered?

Me: No, that was Archibald Cameron . . . Look, this is Alastair

MacDonnell of Glengarry. He spied on Bonnie Prince Charlie

and he went as Pickle the Spy.

John: Who the spy?

Me: Pickle.

John: Interesting. Lovely jacket.

Me: It's a brilliant painting . . . Oh, look at this one!

John: Who is this?

Me: [*reads*] Patrick Grant. A weaver, tailor and tenant farmer.

             Took part in the 1745 Jacobite rising.

John: I bet you it's dead like him. He's got very nice manicured nails.

             Look at his nails.

Me: I read about this guy before. He walked back from Carlisle

             when he went south with Bonnie Prince Charlie and they got

             beat. He came back and was given a pension.

John: Yes?

Me: He lived for a long, long time and became well known as a

             curiosity. Oh, no, this is a different guy. [*reads*] He was

             introduced in person to George IV, his majesty's oldest enemy,

             when the King visited

             Edinburgh in 1822.

             But the old veteran of

             Culloden was given a

             royal pension of a

             guinea a week.

John: That must have been

             a fortune then! Well,

             good on him for

             fighting at

             Culloden . . .

             Oh, here is Flora

Flora MacDonald by Richard Wilson

MacDonald. [*reads*] She helped Prince Charles escape
capture after his defeat at Culloden. They disguised the prince
as her maid and they left in a small boat just as the militia were
closing in.

Me: Charles got rescued by a French ship. Flora got arrested
and taken to London, where she was placed under house
arrest.

John: She's got a nice, smiley face, though.

Me: She ended up in Canada, I think, or America.

John: Yes.

Me: Without Charlie, who disappeared into Europe. Now let's walk
through and see some more modern stuff . . . Is this
photograph James McAvoy?

John: Oh, so it is. Who took it?

Me: Eva Vermandel.

John: It's a bit like him. I met him. He told me that he once
auditioned for me and I turned him down.

Me: Oh! Did you?

John: I must have. He's a wonderful actor but I don't remember him
coming to see me.

Me: Right. Is this one Rikki Fulton?

John: It is, looking for all my life like Rikki Fulton. Who's it by?

Me: Let me see . . . Thomas Kluge, acrylic on canvas.

John: It looks like a photograph. He's verging on an explosion
of laughter.

Me: Look, there's Kirsty Wark over there.

John: Aye.

Me: Kirsty Wark has started a revolution in political commentary. It's all women, now. An amazing number of women are doing political commentary on television now, all started by her.

John: I know, because she's very bright. And here's . . . oh, dear God . . .

Me: Your self-portrait! It's brilliant!

John: The thing was . . . *I always looked like that.* I mean, exactly like Frank Zappa. In 1972 I was in Los Angeles on the Sunset Strip and this tall black guy came over and said, 'Hey, Frank, you remember when we played with the Muscle Shoals?'

Me: Really?

John: I kept trying to tell him he had the wrong guy but he wouldn't listen. Then he went off. Anyway, it was B. B. King.

Me: Ha!

John: Then I went into a drugstore and Al Kooper was there and he said, 'Hey, Frank!' And I thought, Oh, I've had enough of this palaver!

Me: Oh, here's your drawing of Tilda.

John: Aye. I did it in less than twenty minutes. I just mussed up her hair and scribbled it down.

Me: It's colossal. The life in it is amazing.

John: Well, it's pretty lively because I was on edge because she had to go out and was about to bolt out the door at any minute. Right, where's my painting of you? Oh, there you are.

Me: There I are.

John: Who did I paint that for again?

Me: It was a Sunday newspaper, wasn't it?

John: Yes . . . was it the *Sunday Herald*?

Me: I think so.

John: So do I. They went out of business, the *Sunday Herald* – or are they still going?

Me: I don't know. I remember when you painted my live album sleeve.

John: Well, I painted you first.

Me: Yes. You had this idea to paint me, paint the song track names on my body, paint my fingers, everything. You painted me in your studio – that garage behind your house. Then we drove into Glasgow, with me all painted. And it all flaked off.

John: It was all wrong. I should have just painted the sleeve to start with. Then I designed all your wellies when you did The Great Northern Welly Boot Show at Edinburgh Festival.

John Byrne's Glasgow mural for my 75th birthday

Me: Yes. The reggae welly!

John: The wishing welly, with a bucket hanging off it.

Me: My favourite was the Nurse Grant surgical welly. It was an
         evening welly, with satin lapels.

John: And a wee bow tie on the front of it.

Me: Wellies were such a mark of the working class.

John: Aye. What you did was, you turned your wellies down and you
         wore short trousers, and your wellies made welts around
         your calves.

Me: Yeah, and your short trousers made welts on your thighs. You
         had the two rings.

John: Oh, my God! It was torture. Torment. There was no known
         cure. You'd see all the weans with their red rings in the
         summer.

Me: It was known as scurvy.

John: Then later you and I did your big banana boots . . . do you
         remember that Scottish children's rhyme?

Me: *Skinny Malinky long legs, big banana feet . . .*

John: *Went to the pictures and fell through the seat*
         When the picture started . . .

Me: *Skinny Malinky farted . . .*

John: *Skinny Malinky got long legs, big banana feet.*

Me: I think we might have got a wee bit off the topic of fine
         art, here?

'I NEEDED SOMEWHERE TO PARK MA BIKE'

I had made my name in the Humblebums with my storytelling and my comedy routines between the songs, but after Gerry and I split, I still thought of myself as primarily a folk singer who told jokes. There was a guy at our record label, Nat Joseph, who had worked with Hamish Imlach, and who encouraged me to go more for the comedy side of things in the way that Hamish had but, in my mind, I was a musician. My storytelling stuff was still new and growing and I never went on stage with the first idea of what I was going to say. Often, somebody might just tell me a joke then I'd tell it to the crowd in an extended fashion.

This happened to me one night when I was drinking in the Scotia Bar and a pal called Tam Quinn, who played guitar in a band, wandered in and told me a wee joke. He said, 'Jesus's apostles were eating a Chinese takeaway when Jesus came in. Jesus asked them, "Where did you get that?" and they said, "Oh, Judas bought it. He seems to have come into some money." ' I thought it was the funniest thing I had ever heard and I told it onstage that night with some little added bits. It went down extremely well.

I was very encouraged by this, so I started to tell it at every show and expand on it. As a way of introducing it, I said that there had been a terrible mistake and there was a misprint in the Bible – Jesus hadn't really been born in Galilee but in Gallowgate, in the middle of Glasgow, and the Last Supper had taken place in the Sarrie Heid. I kept on expanding and developing it and adding dialogue. I called Jesus 'The Big Yin', which is Scottish for the Big One:

> *The Big Yin came in with his long dress and his casual sandals and his aura: 'Ah, I've been all morning doing miracles, I'm knackered – gies a glass o' that wine!' . . .*

> *They all sat down at a long table, 'cause they were having trouble standing up. You might have seen the picture – the Big Yin is holding on to the table 'cause he's steamin' . . .*

> *The Big Yin says, 'See you, Judas, you're getting on ma tits!' . . .*

> *'Ah, man!' the Big Yin yells, when he wakes up. 'Some joker has nailed me to the wood! Stole my good dress and pawned it and left me lying here in ma Y-fronts . . .'*

I kept adding bits to the Last Supper and Crucifixion story until it was about twenty-five minutes long, and it got me noticed. People started talking about it and came from miles away to see me do it. It became hugely popular and it came to define me. It was the most extraordinary moment of my life, as far as comedy goes. But I had no idea any of that stuff would happen. I just thought it was funny.

After the Last Supper sketch everything just grew and grew for me, over the next few weeks and months and years, and I sometimes think everything I've become since was because of that. That was the first huge break for me. I understand that they are now thinking of putting a blue plaque in the Sarrie Heid about it. I hope it just says:

THIS IS WHERE
THE LAST SUPPER
REALLY HAPPENED

One of my first experiences of hearing Scottish accents on the TV or the radio as a lad had been comedians. When I was very little, there were no Scottish voices on the BBC: it was all just posh English people. That began to change a little bit in the Fifties when two Scottish comedians, Jimmy Logan and Stanley Baxter, had a radio show called *It's All Yours* on the BBC's Scottish Home Service. I thought they were very funny. They had catchphrases: *'If you want your thingummy, ring me,'* or *'Sausages are the boys!'* I don't really much care for catchphrases now, but as a wee boy I thought they were great.

But the first Scottish comedian I really loved was Chic Murray.

He was a Glaswegian guy who always wore a tartan flat cap and he was a sensation. He was well ahead of his time. He used to crack me up with jokes like, 'I was in the Olympic Village and a guy came walking towards me with a big stick on his shoulder. I said, "Are you a pole vaulter?" He said, "No, I'm a German, and don't call me Walter!"' Or he would say, 'The landlady opened the door in her dressing gown. I thought, what a strange place for a door!' I loved the way that Chic used language.

The first time I ever saw Chic was on TV, doing a joke about simmets and drawers (two Scottish words for underpants) that had me on the floor, but he wasn't that good on the telly. Comedians weren't: they used to call them front-of-cloth men because they'd only be given two or three minutes in front of the stage curtain while the main attraction, usually a singer, got ready. Chic was best in the theatre, telling jokes like, 'A neighbour put his budgie in a mincing machine and invented Shredded Tweet.' Or, 'I met a cowboy in a brown paper hat, brown paper waistcoat and brown paper trousers. He was wanted for rustling.'

He was a colossal comedian. I had such respect for him. Years later, when I was starting to get famous, I was interviewed on TV about comedy, and I said, 'If I could ever be half as good as Chic Murray, I'd be amazed.' His daughter, Annabel, was watching, and phoned me and said, 'Would you like to meet him?' It was great to become his friend, because he had set such a benchmark for Scottish comedy. After Chic died, I gave Annabel away when she got married.

COMEDY

Another Scottish comedian I liked when I was young was a guy called Jack Radcliffe. He did this great drunk walk where he only moved one leg and kept the other leg static. Years later I copied that walk when I started doing my own routine taking the piss out of the gallus singers Flo and I had heard in Drumchapel. Once, when I was in the shipyard, Jack Radcliffe turned up out of the blue to do publicity photographs there, and I was really excited to see him.

Yet it was weird. Chic Murray and Jack Radcliffe were great but they were of a different era from me. They were my father's age; from his generation. There was nobody my age telling jokes and being funny in the very early Seventies. There was certainly nobody Scottish or, at least, nobody I was aware of. I knew that I wanted to be a comedian and to tell stories but I wasn't sure how to go about it. I'd seen guys in the folk clubs who called themselves storytellers in the great Scottish tradition of the *seanchaidh*: the oral passers-on of history. They were absolutely fucking shite. They were always these kind of semi-middle-class social workers telling worthy, tedious tales with a prepared beginning, middle and end, and no improvisation at all. They would tell them to children and the children would sit there, bored shitless. I couldn't blame them. I felt totally the same.

Then on the television there were these shows like *The Comedians*, which were very north of England and had all these guys with Perry Como haircuts, in blue mohair suits with velvet pockets, telling racist jokes. Even the black comedians were racist. The worst of the white guys was a big cunt named Bernard Manning. He would come out with this disgusting stuff, like, 'What's another name for a toilet? A Pakistani washing machine!'

I had no time for that rubbish. I was coming from my folky, hippy, peace-and-love background and I saw racism like that for what it was – fascism. Those guys were scared to be anti-Semitic because they knew that Jews have got balls and would come back at them. They wouldn't have let them get away with it, whereas they knew that the Pakistani community would just shrug it off. It was very wrong and I was utterly against it.

I wasn't part of that world. I was hairy and hippy-looking and I knew I wouldn't be welcome on the variety club circuit that they all played. I couldn't stand their stupid jokes about their mothers-in-law and how Irish people were all thick – didn't they know that Ireland produces more great writers per head than any other country in the world? I didn't want to be like those wankers but at the time I didn't have any other guidelines on how to be a comedian.

Now and then I'd meet an older comedian or comic writer and they would give me bits of advice. I remember one guy telling me, 'Spam is funny, sausages are funny, Partick Thistle is funny.' I didn't want all that crap. I never did a Spam joke or a Partick This-tle joke in my life.* Those old-school comedians were coming

---

* Well, actually, I *did* do one Partick Thistle joke. It was about listening to the football scores on a Saturday night, and saying, 'Is that their full name, Partick

from cabaret, or from TV and radio, where they would have six or eight minutes and would have to clear in advance exactly what they were going to say. I had a totally different background. I came from the folk world, where there were no rules and I was completely free to say what I wanted at any length I wanted to. I wanted to go somewhere else with comedy, to get deep into ordinary life, and how people thought and talked, and politics, and to kind of be a commentator on the society that I lived in.

My influences were those other guys in the Scottish folk world that I loved, like Hamish Imlach and Matt McGinn, and the English guys like Jasper Carrott and Mike Harding, who were doing personal stuff and political stuff and generally *just talking* about whatever took their fancy. I wanted to emulate them and, even beyond that, I wanted to emulate the guys I'd met in the shipyards, the patter merchants who had made me howl with laughter. These were all guys who were being funny without telling jokes: who were funny about everyday things all around them and who took the piss out of people relentlessly. They refused to take life too seriously because they knew that you can volunteer to do that but it's going to bite you on the arse. Because working-class life is harsh, and you can either break down and complain about how miserable your life is, or you can *have a go at it* and survive. And that's the basis of what I do.

Thistle Nil? Only that's what I hear every week!' The Partick Thistle fans hated it but I couldn't resist – it was a good joke.

So, I just carried on doing shows where I was singing funny songs on the banjo and generally just *chatting* the same way I would chat to a mate in the shipyard or the pub. I would start to tell a joke, then get distracted into anecdotal stuff, then pick up the joke again, which felt perfectly natural to me. For some reason, people seemed to find it hysterically funny that I could leave a story for five or six minutes and then come back to it. I would try to explain to them: 'When you talk to your pals in the street, you don't proceed logically from one to ten in your conversation. It's not A-B-C. The conversation wanders off and has a look around, and you change the subject when things occur to you! *That's* all I'm doing.'

I didn't have a technique for changing the subject. That's not how my brain works. I would be talking about something in the joke and it would remind me of something else and I'd go off on a limb then come back again. My theory, if I had one, was to keep talking until I remembered what it was that I was talking about. That was about as deep as it got. It was a mystery to me where it was all coming from. I never had notes, or a script. I might have a scrap of paper with a few words on it.

Nowadays, I have a stool with a glass top on stage, and it has my headlines on it. It might just say:

ARMY

BROKE

And that's it. Lenny Henry told me he thought I had a computer with all my routines stored on it, but I havenae. I've always worked the same way, and happily, people seem to like it.

Back in the early days, I would talk about Glasgow accents, and jobbies, and farting. I would describe being in the cinema and being desperate to fart and trying to get out of the row to go and fart somewhere, and how you have to walk all stiff-legged because your bum is passing people's faces. I'd get wilder and talk about sex, because anywhere that people are vulnerable they are funny, and you're never more vulnerable than when your trousers are around your ankles.

I had learned from listening to Chic Murray that if you did stuff that people related to, recognisably Scottish or Glaswegian stuff, they loved it. There was a phenomenon when I played that, instead of telling a story and doing a punchline and getting a laugh, I would get lots of ripples of laughter as I went along, building up the story. This soon became like an addiction to me, or a disease, and I couldn't get enough of it. I couldn't live without it.

I would go on intending to say something and never get around to it. I got quite famous for forgetting to announce people's birthdays, but it wasn't deliberate. I would get given all sorts of requests and I'd intend to do them but when I got out there, I'd completely forget because I was intent on saying something else. I was just going on stage and inventing stuff, which is what has made my name, but even now I find it difficult to analyse or describe how it works.

I didn't think that I had invented a new realm of comedy, though. That never occurred to me. I remember once, at the start, playing at Glasgow Art School to a very middle-class crowd and it being profoundly different. Being accepted by those guys was spectacular.

'That was amazing, it was so organic!' they told me, when I came off the stage.

'What?' I said.

'Your comedy, and the way you talk about things, is organic!'

I had no idea what they were on about but I thought, *Oh, I've done myself a bit of good here!*

I waved my hands around a lot while I was onstage. I mimed things and acted them out. Again, I never thought about it – I just did it because that was what the stories needed. I've always been very expressive with my hands. I used to go out to pubs or cafés with my pals, and there was one girl who used to grab my hands while I was telling a story, hold them still, and say, 'See? You can't talk without them, can you?' I used to get quite offended, but now I think she was probably right.

I soon started becoming known as the Big Yin. There were a couple of reasons for that. One was the Last Supper sketch but another was that I did a thing where I became my own heckler. I would do a spot of gallus singing and then heckle myself: 'Jesus, no more wine in that room! Give us a bit of silence there, Big Yin!'

I was calling myself the Big Yin and it caught on. Other people started saying it.

The funny thing was that when I was a kid, I was called Wee Billy to differentiate me from my dad, who was also Billy and was a giant of a man. Then I grew bigger than him, and also became known as the Big Yin in Scotland, so it got totally confusing. Our friends would have conversations like this in the pub:

'Billy Connolly was just in.'

'Oh? Big Billy or Wee Billy?'

'The Big Yin.'

'Oh, Wee Billy!'

I imagine that any stranger wandering into that pub would have wondered, *What the fuck are these people talking about?*

The other thing that I became known for, of course, was swearing. This wasn't intentional. The first time I ever swore on stage, it was an accident. It just slipped out: 'Ah, for fuck's sake!' But I'll never forget how the audience reacted to it. They just all fell back in a huge wave of laughter that went on and on and on. They were relieved to hear a comedian who spoke the same way as they spoke and who said what they said. So, I kept the swearing in. It's a potent weapon. Glaswegians are like New Yorkers – we swear very, very well. It's got that same *boom, boom, boom* effect as when New Yorkers say, 'Motherfucker!' It's a drum beat and it hits you where you live. It's powerful.

Let me give you my thoughts on swearing. I swear when it makes a joke stronger. I'm not proud of it but I'm not ashamed of it, either. It's just language and I don't know what the panic is about. It's all part of the poetry of working-class speech. There's a lot of snobbery about swearing. People swear in movies, and apparently that is all fine and dandy. When toffs swear, it's OK, even though toffs don't swear very well: 'Bloody get your bloody thing off that bloody thing!' But when working-class people swear, it's regarded as nasty.

Glaswegian is very guttural and harsh. There is no question what you are talking about when you are swearing. There's a particular swearing expression in Glasgow that is quite poetic and quite violent as well and I've never heard it anywhere else. If something goes wrong, people just say, 'Jesus suffering fuck!' Now, *that* is poetry, whether you like it or not. You have to stand back and admit that the absolute correct thing has just been uttered. 'Jesus suffering fuck!' just does it to me. The number of times I have seen people coming in doors and discovering something and saying, 'Oh, Jesus suffering fuck!' It can mean, 'Who moved my equipment?' 'Who peed where I'm working?' 'Who stole my jacket?' It can mean anything. It's just fucking brilliant. *That's* the kind of swearing I like.

It's like, 'What the fuck?' when something catastrophic has occurred. There is no equivalent expression for 'What the fuck?' Nor is there any need for anything else to be said, or to add anything to it. You don't get people saying, 'What the fuck . . . is going on here?' You only need the first three words. In fact, when you're writing it, you only need the first three letters: 'WTF?'

It's perfect. 'Fuck off' is the same. It's one of the most perfect statements there is: 'I want you to try harder!' 'Fuck off!' It's multi-lingual: you can say it in any country and they will understand what you are saying. You might be at Lhasa Gonggar Airport in Tibet and notice somebody fucking around with your luggage. You can say, 'Hey, you!'

'Who, me?'

'Aye, Baldy. Fuck off!'

You never get them saying, 'Pardon? Can you explain that?' It's just 'Fuck off!' and you can watch him as off he fucks. That guttural 'k' – it's all self-explanatory.

By the same token, there's no equivalent for fucked:

'What do you think of this weather?'

'It's fucked.'

'What's that job like up there?'

'It's fucked. It was OK a while ago, but it's fucked now.'

The way I feel about swearing was summed up by an interview I heard with a Scottish author named James Kelman, who wrote a book called *How Late It Was, How Late*. He swears a lot in his books and the woman who was interviewing him said, 'I'm surprised you don't swear as much as you do in your books.' He said, 'I *do*, I just don't happen to feel like it right now.' He explained: 'I don't *have* to swear – if you show me a non-swearing equivalent for "fucking beautiful!", I will use it. But sometimes, maybe at the football, it's just perfect, and nothing else will do – "Fucking beautiful!" '

I'm the same. I don't *have* to swear and I can understand why some people get offended by it. *I* can get irritated by it, if somebody in a restaurant or on a bus is swearing loudly and annoying people. I have no good reason for swearing and I have no good reason for *not* doing it. But I think we're better for it. Life is more honest with swearing than it is without it.

I have to say I have never liked anybody who is pushed as being a 'clean entertainer' or a 'family entertainer'. It generally means that they're shit. *'He doesnae swear, he doesnae offend'* – well, chances are he doesnae entertain! I have yet to meet anybody who is both a clean, family entertainer and a good comedian. At one end, you've got the family entertainers who never swear, and at the other end, you've got comics like Frankie Boyle, who is great. He knows about swearing. The Frankie Boyles of this world are really necessary. They show you where the middle is by being extreme.

Language is so important in comedy and it can be so funny in everyday life.* 'Cunt' is a serious word, though. People get deeply wounded by it. One day my brother-in-law told me he'd been on the escalator in Littlewood's on Argyle Street and he'd heard a guy casually say to his mate, 'Aye, there are a lot of English cunts in here!' I lost my balance from laughing when I heard that. Then I was watching Frankie Boyle on TV recently and a guy on his show

---

* I remember Michael Caine telling me that his father, who was a fish market porter, couldn't say the word 'Welsh' without saying 'git' after it. So, he would come home from the market and tell his family, 'We've got a really nice Welsh git working with us at the minute!'

said, 'Ah, he's a cunt!' I was shocked. I thought, oh Jesus! Saying 'cunt' on television! But then I thought again: *Eh, hang on, I'm Billy Connolly!* I'm not sure I'm in any position to be offended here!

Anyway . . . where was I?

Despite the swearing, or maybe because of it, I was slowly getting better known in Glasgow and around Scotland and playing bigger venues when I went out on tour. They weren't all folk music fans. By now, people were coming mostly for the comedy – and yet despite this, I was still thinking of myself as a musician. It was just how I regarded myself. I still took my banjo to every show and walked onstage carrying it. It didn't make any difference to my way of thinking that I was playing it less and less, and that at some shows I hardly picked it up at all. I guess by then it wasn't much more than a prop, but psychologically, I couldn't do without my banjo and it didn't even occur to me to try.

Then, one night, I forgot it. I drove to a gig and when I got there, I went to fetch my banjo and it wasn't there – I had left it in my hotel. I had to do the gig without it, and before I went on, I was actually trembling. I felt like I was naked. But I made it through the show just fine, and after that I'd take the banjo to the gigs but leave it on the side of the stage.

I remember the first Scottish gig where I deliberately left the banjo in the wings was in Forfar in the early Seventies. That was also the first gig where I didn't use an upright microphone. I had always used an old-fashioned upright mic, on a stand, but then

I started wearing one on my body as well to allow me to walk around the stage. I started off taking tentative little steps away from the mic stand, then as I grew more confident about using my body mic, I'd walk further and further away from the stand. Then I got rid of the upright mic completely and prowled the stage like an animal. I was releasing myself from the bonds of the old style. I even started seeing people copying me and doing the same thing, and that made me feel quite proud.

As I got better known, my outfits got wilder and wilder. I had some amazing stage clothes. I had velvet and satin suits made, in pink or garish red and purple, with Lurex stars on the arse. I bought T-shirts with tails. I wore knitted leotards, including one that was a big pair of scissors, with my arms as the handles and my legs as the blades. They used to drive me insane with itch. One leotard had my face on the bum and if I moved my arse, my hair swung. I bought fur coats from Paddy's Market in Glasgow, took the linings out, wore the coats inside-out and drew on the fur with felt-tip markers.

There was a thinking behind all this, which was, *don't dress for what you're doing*. I've always thought if there is somebody in an audience who has never seen me before, I don't want to give him any clues. I don't want to walk on like a comedian, wearing something funny like a funny slogan or a funny picture. This guy might not know if I'm an acrobat or a magician or a comedian. It's a great place for me to start from.

I figured, if people were looking at me on stage, wondering

What's this? before I even started to talk, I had them, like a posses-
sion. I could mould them and take them with me on my story. So,
when my hair was big and fluffy, I used to get it lit up from behind
in different colours. It was a big dramatic effect and like rock and
roll rather than comedy. It drew people in and it took them to
another place they didn't know they were going to. If I were just a
guy with his jacket sleeves rolled up, they might feel like we were
all in a student union and they could heckle me.

Students tended to like what I was doing back in the early days
but the feeling wasnae always mutual. There were too many college gigs where the students just heckled me all night or threw up
in my banjo case. I had had enough of it one night when my manager at the time, a Glaswegian guy named Frank Lynch, booked
me against my wishes to play Glasgow University. As soon as I walked
on, a voice from the crowd yelled, 'Get off!' 'Certainly!' I replied,
turned right around, and walked offstage and home. That was the
end of that gig.

I started doing little bits of TV. A guy called Bill Tennent used
to host a talk show on STV called *Dateline* and any time that somebody more important dropped out at the last minute, or he was
struggling to fill a slot, he would invite me on to play my banjo and
sing a wee song. Then one day he had an emergency and asked me
if I would be a proper interview guest. It went well and I got a few
laughs and after it finished, as we went off the air, Bill leaned
forwards, tapped me on the knee and quietly told me: 'You did
yourself some good there.'

I had a couple of landmark moments that really helped to make my comedy career. The first was the Last Supper and Crucifixion and the second came when my A&R supporter at Transatlantic Records, Nat Joseph, put out a couple of albums of my live shows: *Billy Connolly Live!* and *Solo Concert.* This was a seriously bold move for a comedian that hardly anybody had heard of outside of Glasgow, but it got people interested in me. One weird thing with those albums was that because of the swearing and stuff like '*See you, Judas, you're getting on my tits!*' they were regarded as rebellious, like rock and roll albums. Some radio stations banned them and a lot of people have told me that, when they were kids, they would sneak the records on and play them without their parents knowing. They identified with them as *being for them,* just as I had with 'Heartbreak Hotel' and Hank Williams.

And, in 1975, those albums got me my second big break. Michael Parkinson was up in Glasgow getting a taxi to the airport, and his taxi driver recognised him, stopped the cab at a record shop to buy one of my records and insisted that he listened to it when he got home. Parky didn't play it straight away, but when he did he liked it so much that he booked me for his television chat show.

Parkinson was a huge deal in those days, going out to ten million people on BBC1 live on a Saturday evening, and on our way down to appear on the programme, my manager, Frank, had one piece of advice for me: 'Billy, whatever you do, don't tell him the joke about the dead wife and her arse!' Well, I meant to follow his sage warning, but when the show started, I felt the interview was going so well that I decided to chance my arm. 'I hope I can get away with this one, it's a beauty!' I told Parkinson, who looked a wee bit wary, and I fired into the joke:

'This guy was going to meet his friend in the pub. He says, "How's it going?" and he says, "Fine, fine." He says, "How's the wife?" and the guy says, "Oh, she's deid. I murdered her." He says, "You're kidding me on?" and he says, "No, no, this morning. I'll show you if you want." "Aye, show me." So, they go away up to his tenement building, into the back green, into the wash house, and sure enough there's a big mound of earth, and there's a bum sticking out of it. He says, "Is that her?" "Aye." He says, "What did you leave her bum sticking out for?" And he says, "I needed somewhere to park ma bike."'

As the credits rolled at the end of the show, Parky leaned forward and told me exactly the same thing that Bill Tennent had said on *Dateline*: 'You did yourself some good there.' It was the strangest thing.

It's hard to believe now because it's a pretty tame wee joke in the grand scheme of things, but in 1975 my bum story took the country by storm. On the morning after the show I went to Heathrow Airport to fly home and a Chinese guy asked me for my autograph. I thought, *Well, that's a bit different.* When I got off the plane at the other end and walked through Glasgow Airport, all the people in the airport applauded me. I thought, *Oh God, I think I might have done something here. This is a lot bigger than I imagined.* I had gone up a step in my fame and it kind of overwhelmed me for a bit. After my first *Parkinson* appearance, my concerts began selling out in an instant and I was playing bigger and bigger venues: King's Theatre, Pavilion Theatre, Carnegie Hall. I started playing more shows in England and Wales and Ireland, as well as Scotland, and then I started getting international gigs: Australia, Canada, America.

This meant playing to people who might struggle with the Scottish accent. People often tell me that when they hear my old stuff like the Last Supper sketch, they have trouble telling what I'm saying if they're not from Scotland – in fact, if they're not from Partick! They say that I speak a lot clearer now and they ask me if I deliberately changed the way I talk, and if I was ever advised that I needed to. The answer is, no, I didnae and I wasnae. I suppose that I just started actually moving my lips when I speak. A lot of Glaswegians don't do that. When they talk, their lips are like the slot in a postbox. They use half-words, and they let their sentences fall away at the end, and it confuses the fuck out of people. A Scotsman will often say, 'I had to slow down in order to be understood,' but, to me, it's not really a question of slowing down. It's a question of clarity.*

---

* When I first started seeing Pamela, and she came to Glasgow with me, we went to a curry house. The Indian waiter had shoes that turned up at the front and a turban with a gem on it – the whole nine yards. He came right over to our table and said, 'Aye, Billy, wot aboot Celtic, eh?!' and started banging on in broad Glaswegian about how great Celtic were. Pamela slid under the table. She had never seen anything like it.

COMEDY

· · · · · · · ·

Half a century since I started telling jokes on stage, I feel lucky that my success has never really waned. It has gone up and up and up all the time, until I have found myself playing indoor arenas and even stadiums. The venues have got bigger but I've never really changed what I do. My comedy is all about observing people leading their day-to-day lives and finding what is funny in them and about them. It's a question of letting the ordinary things that happen to us *mean something*. Like I said, life can be tough, and you either give up and moan about it, or you *have a go at it*.

I love laughing at things until I lose control and my body doesn't work any more. My son, Jamie, can do that to me. We were away fishing a while ago and he told me a story that a female friend had told him about her son having a tick on the end of his penis. Her husband was away with work but she thought he would know what to do, so she phoned him up. Her husband said, 'Get Vaseline and rub it on his penis, get a grip of the tick with tweezers and twist it out, pulling all the time.' Well, the mother went away to get Vaseline but couldn't find any so she put Vicks VapoRub on her son's willy instead, twisting away with the tweezers at the same time. The poor screaming lad nearly passed out with the pain of it. Jamie told me that story and I lost control completely. I was hanging helplessly off my fishing chair and he had to hold me up. And *that* is the best feeling in the world.

I don't think I have anything as poncey as a philosophy of my comedy but I can tell you a nice wee story that perfectly illustrates the kind of thing that I love to observe and then to talk about.

Molly Weir, the Glaswegian actress, told it to me. Molly was famous for being in the 1950s radio sitcom *Life with the Lyons*, and she was also well known for being in TV adverts in the 1970s for Flash disinfectant. She had this great, nasal Scottish accent: 'Aye – Flash cleans baths without scratching!' She was a lovely woman – I did *Any Questions* on the radio with her once. She's long dead, now. Molly told me she had been to Saltcoats, which is near Ardrossan, down on the Clyde, and she described a little scene she had witnessed there, which means a lot to me:

There was a woman, a tired housewife, sitting on the beach at Saltcoats on a chair from her home. It wasn't a deckchair, it was a proper chair from the kitchen. She had a newspaper over her face and was obviously a knackered housewife taking a break and taking the air.

Her children were playing in the sand and her daughter came running up to her: 'Mummy, Mummy!' From under the newspaper came a tired voice: 'What is it?' 'Mummy, Johnny won't eat his sandwich, he wants to eat his chocolate biscuit first.' The mum said, 'Tell him to eat his sandwich first before he eats his chocolate biscuit.' The girl ran away then came back.

'Mummy, Mummy, he says he's not going to eat his sandwich first, he's going to eat his chocolate biscuit. He hates his sandwich.' 'Tell him to eat his sandwich first.' The daughter ran away again. She came back: 'Mummy, Mummy!' 'What is it?' said the exhausted woman, still under her newspaper. 'Mummy, Mummy, he says he doesn't care what you say, he's going to eat his chocolate biscuit. He doesn't want his sandwich.'

'Tell him to eat his sandwich first.' The girl came back one more time. 'Mummy, Mummy!' 'What is it?' 'He's flung his sandwich in the Clyde and he's ate his chocolate biscuit!' And the tired voice from under the newspaper said: 'Hit him.'

That to me is *everything*. That's where I come from. That's where I was brought up. That's the lessons I learned. It's all encapsulated in that one little thing: *'Hit him.'* Because she could just as easily have said, 'Oh, I'm so fucked!'

That's what you do if you're a comedian. You recognise what is going on around you and you make it funny. It's the same thing that people do when they're eating their dinner at nights. They talk about politics or whatever, things they have seen during the day, and they try to be funny about them. It's hard to explain what I do, in a way. It's hard to explain why you're doing anything in show business. I tell jokes and am funny at such-and-such a place one night, then I do it again at a different place the next night. Compared to what everybody else does every day, it's kind of nothing – but it's a great thing, as well.

I've been famous as a comedian a very long time and I like it because I like being good at it. It's the same as I felt when I was a welder: I liked being good at that too. I never felt I was good as a football player because I was terrible, but as a comedian, without being cocky, I feel that my fame is deserved. On the very best nights, I'll come off stage and think, *I wish I was in the audience tonight.*

The bottom line is still that I love making people laugh. I love hitting a crowd with a smart one and hearing them roar. I don't know what it is, I don't know how I do it, it just comes to me and I do it and the room explodes. It's a magic thing to have: it's like waving a magic wand. It brings good in the room and it relaxes everybody. And I would like to carry on doing it until I can't do it any more.

'Getting Old Isn't Funny, Is It?' . . . A Conversation on Living with Parkinson's

In 2012, I was diagnosed with Parkinson's disease. I found out about it in the strangest way. I was staying in a hotel in Los Angeles and had been coming and going in and out of the lobby. There was an Australian dance team staying there, and the guy in charge of them came over to me and said, 'Billy, I'm a fan of yours and I'm a doctor. I've been watching you walking in and out of here and you have a strange gait. I think you have got early onset Parkinson's disease. You need to go and see your doctor.' When I got back home I went to see the doctor and he did blood tests and various other little bits and pieces, and he told me that I had it: the guy had been right.

That diagnosis didn't come during the best of weeks for me. In the same week, I was also told that I had gone deaf and that I had prostate cancer. The doctor who broke the prostate news to me – on the same day that I got told about the Parkinson's – said, 'First of all, you're not going to die.' I was shocked, and said, *'Of course I'm not going to fucking die!'* It never crossed my mind.

Those last two ailments are gone now. I have got great wee hearing aids so my hearing isn't a problem and I had successful surgery on my prostate – it was *in and out, done,* as simple as that. But the Parkinson's disease is staying with me. It's never going to go away. I've learned to live with it: I get up every morning and do my exercises, I take my medication, I've learned to take it easier and to look out for when the shaking starts (it's always my left hand). It's the first thing I think of every morning when I wake up . . . but I'm coping with it and I'm hanging in there.

There is a lot of work being done to try to find a cure for Parkinson's and one of the world's best research scientists is in Scotland. Sir Ian Wilmut is chair of the Scottish Centre for Regenerative Medicine at Edinburgh University and is renowned around the globe for being the first scientist to clone a mammal when he and his team cloned Dolly the sheep in 1996. Sir Ian's team are researching cures for Parkinson's, motor neuron disease and multiple sclerosis – and he was himself diagnosed with Parkinson's just before Christmas 2017. We talked about Dolly Parton, hairy ears, and learning to live with the shakes.

With Sir Ian in Edinburgh

Sir Ian: Billy, really pleased to meet you.

Me: Great, it's a joy to meet you.

Sir Ian: I'm just sorry about the circumstances that we meet in.

Me: With the Parkinson's?

Sir Ian: Yes. This dreadful disease that we both have.

Me: Yes. We will talk a lot more about this shortly – but first, I want to ask you about Dolly the sheep. What was your aim when you cloned her?

Sir Ian: Well, when we started cloning Dolly we were actually doing it from a point of view of farm-animal science. If we could take cells from embryos and grow them, we might be able to make genetic changes in the cells. By the time we'd got Dolly we realised that we'd overturned a rule of biology. What people used to think was that once a cell had developed, it was fixed, it couldn't be changed. Whereas Dolly showed that the cells can change.

Me: Did you really name Dolly after Dolly Parton?

Sir Ian: Yes. The mothers of the clones sometimes had real difficulty giving birth so we had somebody with the pregnant sheep twenty-four hours a day, seven days a week. The pregnancies ran from October through to March so those guys were sitting with them night and day for months. It was incredibly boring and two of them, sitting there one night, started saying, 'Where did that cell come from? It came from the mammary gland of a ewe.'

Me: A-ha!

Sir Ian: That was the trigger. If you're thinking 'mammary gland', who do you think of first? Dolly Parton. When we finally produced Dolly, Dolly Parton's manager was reported to have said, 'There's no such thing as baa-d publicity.'

Me: That's very good.

Sir Ian: I think it gave us an aura of humanity.

Me: Absolutely. Did you the world of good, I should imagine.

Sir Ian: Yes.

Me: Better than naming it after some dreary old churchman. How did it feel being the first ever to do what you did?

Sir Ian: Great.

Me: I would imagine so. I was recently watching *Antiques Roadshow* and the lady who presents it, Fiona Bruce, came on at the end with a phial and said, 'This is an antique of the future. It's three drops of Dolly's blood.' How do you feel about that?

Sir Ian: I'd want to know how she knows. It might be anything!

Me: Yes, that's right. It might be tomato sauce.

Sir Ian: Exactly, but if somebody can make some money from it, all well and good. So, how are you coping with the Parkinson's?

Me: I've got, kind of, used to it. You never really get used to it but I wake up with it every day and *I wear it.*

Sir Ian: Yes. Mine was detected just before Christmas last year so I'm not quite so badly affected, yet. You've had it much longer than I have.

Me: Aye. It came as a kind of shock to me when I got it. I had several other things all reported on the same week and it was a shocker.

Sir Ian: Yes, it's not good.

Me: Are you working on Parkinson's disease now?

Sir Ian: Some of my colleagues are, yes. I work in the Centre for Regenerative Medicine and Parkinson's, motor neuron disease and multiple sclerosis are the main diseases that my colleagues work on. We are getting to the point where we think we understand enough about what's causing Parkinson's and how we can cure it and are beginning to plan for the first experimental treatments.

A group of scientists in London and Sweden identified some Californians who had damage very similar to Parkinson's from taking drugs. They were cured by taking cells from human foetuses that were being aborted, from the particular part of the brain which is the source of the problem and injecting them into the sufferer's brains.

Me: Yes, I spoke to some scientists at Harvard who were doing that.

Sir Ian: Now we have to refine the process and find another source of cells. There are various kinds of stem cells which will grow indefinitely, producing millions and millions of cells. We're learning to change them to the kind of cells needed to treat Parkinson's so in the end it will be possible to treat millions of patients using cells produced in the lab. It means that one day, maybe, in terms of a treatment for Parkinson's disease, people may take skin from patients, make a useful genetic change, allow them to develop to a useful stage of development and then put them into the brain of the person who has Parkinson's, in just the same way that the original group in Sweden did.

Me: That's great. But don't you get accused of playing God?

Sir Ian: Oh, yes, but I don't really know what that means. If we're able to do something which is useful, even providing a treatment for one person or five people, you know, I think it should be encouraged.

Me: Yes, you're doing it to help people. It's not as if you're creating millions of marching identical men.

Sir Ian: No.

Me: Religious people tend to get in the road of progress all the time.

Sir Ian: Yes.

Me: That baffles me because I thought believing in God and greatness and good would make them optimists, but it doesn't seem to. It tends to make them pessimistic.

Sir Ian: I think it's the puritanism of it, isn't it? That maybe they don't have control of it and there's an anxiety about it.

Me: That's the key, the control. But the ethics of it are quite complicated, aren't they?

Sir Ian: Yes. That's not my field. I'll defer to you.

Me: Oh, I'm the ethics man. As opposed to the Essex Man.

Sir Ian: You'd never be mistaken for an Essex Man.

Me: The work you're doing is great. I'm glad you're around.

Sir Ian: I mainly try to explain it and advertise it and look for funding. That's one reason I made public that I've got Parkinson's. It's great that you've done the same thing. About 70,000 people show the first symptoms of Parkinson's in the UK every year. So, if we can say, 'Look, there are lots of people like us with this disease,' maybe it'll help us get that funding. Because immunologists think that cells carefully selected from just 150 people would provide a reasonable immunological match for the population of the UK.

Me: Wow!

Sir Ian: Yes, and as a philanthropic step that appeals to me. Rather than having a procedure which would probably cost £50,000 to £100,000 each if you did it for an individual, you would have a procedure which could be used to provide everybody with a similar treatment.

Me: That's tremendous.

Sir Ian: You mentioned that you had a number of other bad medical reports at the same time?

Me: Yes.

Sir Ian: Have you got prostate trouble?

Me: Yes. I had to have it removed. I got hearing aids the same week; I went deaf. I just happened to get the report for my deafness in the same week, so I wear hearing aids, now. I'm a shadow of my former self.

Sir Ian:	They don't show.
Me:	No, they don't, I've got hairy ears. Getting old isn't funny, is it?
Sir Ian:	No. No, it's not.
Me:	Nobody warned me about this. Or, if they did, I wasn't listening.
Sir Ian:	Yes.
Me:	You like to hill-walk?
Sir Ian:	I used to, yes. I mean, my feet and legs seem to be most affected.
Me:	Yes. My left arm and left leg aren't the same as my right, any more.
Sir Ian:	Oh, right. Well, no, I'm definitely not affected as badly as that.
Me:	I went to physiotherapy in Florida, where I live, and there's a special course for Parkinson's disease sufferers and I do it every day. It's loosened me up.
Sir Ian:	Right. Good for you having the dedication.
Me:	It's guilt-driven. The Catholic upbringing helps.
Sir Ian:	Yes. I've been to a Pilates class, which I enjoy doing because you're doing particular movements and really stretching.
Me:	I try everything. I get massages and messed around generally. I find it helps me and then that lasts a little while and then I get worse, again. I have to go and do something else as the disease creeps merrily forward. It seems relentless.
Sir Ian:	Yes, it is. The first thing the doctor said to me after convincing himself that I'd got it was: 'You've got between ten and

fifteen years.' I hadn't even asked him. Is that similar to what you were told?

Me: He said I'd live until I was ninety, which is fifteen years left.

Sir Ian: That's good.

Me: Aye. I wasn't expecting to live that long before I got Parkinson's, so I was quite pleased! But we might not make it that far, we're not well men. Sometimes I have trouble getting out of chairs.

Sir Ian: Yes, it's a bit of a surprise to find people helping us up because we are old men.

Me: There are other times that I think I'm being perfectly OK and the guy in the supermarket will say, 'Would you like me to help you out to your car with those groceries?' I think, *I thought I was looking great!*

Sir Ian: Sometimes it's little old women who help.

Me: Absolutely. And I don't drive any more.

Sir Ian: You don't?

Me: But I am thinking of taking it up again. I feel OK about it.

Sir Ian: Well, I don't think you'd have any problems.

Me: That's great. It would be nice to see you getting some benefit from all your experimenting. You know, personally, on your Parkinson's stuff, all your research. And it's been a huge pleasure to meet you.

Sir Ian: Oh, the pleasure's mine. I go back to the days of watching you on *Parkinson* talking about who can pee the highest!

Me: Ah, yes. The other *Parkinson* . . .

'Anybody want to hear "The Polka Dot Blues"? No?'

Visiting Euan Cattanach, another 'Banjo Man', who makes stringed instruments in Aberfeldy, Perthshire

On stage playing autoharp with legendary folk singer Ralph McTell

And the Lord said: 'See you, Judas, you're getting on ma tits!'

My banana boots: people said I was taking the pith

With Rory Gallagher, John Bonham and various other reprobates, filming a TV show in 1980

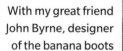

With my great friend John Byrne, designer of the banana boots

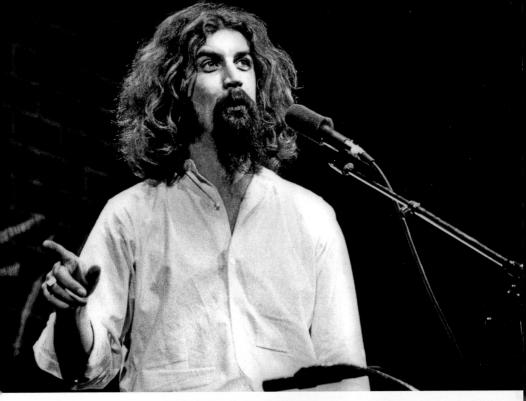

'And another thing ...'
The Big Yin is born

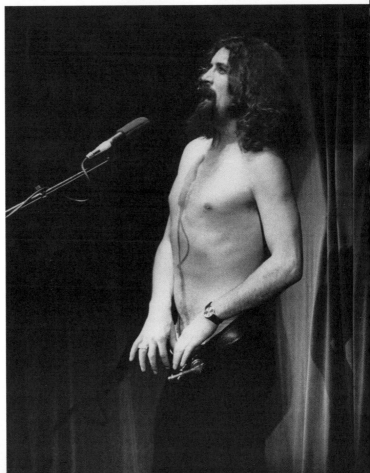

'Anybody want to see
this? No, I thought not ...'

Years ahead of his time: my first comedy hero, Chic Murray

With my sorely missed brother in comedy, Robin Williams

On the High Horse tour after my Parkinson's diagnosis

Abandon hope, all ye who enter here: the infernal St Peter's School for Boys

Bizarrely, the call from Jock Stein never came

Reunited with my Flying Scot bike, fifty years on

With pals: thoughts of my knitted swimming costume traumatise me to this day

Knitted costumes a-go-go at Loch Ard. Filming my 2018 TV series

As a Cub, I pitched many a tent in Milngavie

Singing shortbread tin Sir Harry Lauder, roamin' in the soddin' gloamin'

Holidays began right here: the *Waverley* sets sail for Bute

'What time is it, Billy?' 'Well, the big hand is on ...' CLONK!

Rothesay: a jewel in Scotland's crown, sixty years ago and now

Modern, inclusive Scotland: Syrian refugee Malek Helmi (on my right) and his family have settled in Rothesay and opened a thriving bakery

Is it an armadillo? Is it a croissant? You decide!

Seeing huge murals of me around Glasgow by Rachel Maclean (right), Jack Vettriano (below) and John Byrne was incredibly moving

'THIS IS ALL NONSENSE, I DON'T BELIEVE IT'

People always think of me as being definitively Glaswegian but I am actually part-seal. Back in the mists of time my family name was spelled Connelly, which in Irish mythology are part-seal, part-human beasts who came out of the sea. I had my DNA analysed in 2018 and it is quite a mix. They didn't find any seal, but, apparently, I am 94 per cent from Britain and Ireland (with a wee bit of exotic India on my mum's side – when I did *Who Do You Think You Are?* on TV, I learned that my great-grandmother was born in Bangalore. I love that). And of that 94 per cent, some comes from the west of Scotland, some from Cornwall and some from the west of Ireland. So all from west coasts, which suits me fine. They are what I am drawn towards. Scotland's west coast is one of the most beautiful places on the planet. I don't think I can say that too many times.

My grandfather – my father's dad, Jack – came from Connemara in County Galway, in the west of Ireland, but moved to

Glasgow in the 1920s. He was following on from the influx of Irish into Scotland eighty years earlier during the Great Potato Famine. Those people arrived here barefoot and totally skint and they were consequently looked down upon by the Scottish people. These Irish immigrants, and their sons and daughters, had a lot of faith in their Catholic religion and they used it as a spiritual bulwark against the hatred that they were shown when they came to Scotland.

This all set the scene for the schism that has riven society in Glasgow and Scotland and made everybody take sides for way, way too long: Protestant vs Catholic; blue vs green; Rangers vs Celtic. I had thought for a while that this was disappearing from Scottish life, but now I am not so sure: I sometimes fear it will be with us forever. At least we no longer see the signs that used to hang outside firms with vacancies in the 1930s, when my dad was looking for work: 'NO IRISH NEED APPLY'.

A variation of this was 'APPRENTICES WANTED: BOYS' BRIGADE WELCOME'. As only Protestants were allowed to join this Scouts-like youth organisation, this sign's real meaning was fairly unambiguous.

As a wee infant I was blithely indifferent to sectarian tensions, but it didn't take me too long to become aware of a certain inexplicable stigma that appeared to be attached to us. I would have been about four years old when I was playing in Stewartville Street with a friend, Marie, and her grandad leaned out of their upstairs window, pipe in hand, to admonish her: 'I have told you before about playing with Catholics!' Nor was the prejudice one-sided.

When my Auntie Mona found out, at around the same time, that Florence and I were in the habit of wandering in to a Protestant kids' club called Band of Hope, mainly because we got a free bun and a slide show of the Holy Land, she was equally horrified.

Yet my infant school, St Peter's, was where the big oppressive hand of religion first came crashing down on me. Once I had got over the horror of the life-sized, bleeding crucified Christ in the main foyer, I had to cope with being informed by the nuns that God was dead and it was my fault. I couldn't begin to work out how I had caused all that grief to happen before I had even been born. The pictures of Hell displayed on Sister Philomena's office walls were also a serious headfuck whenever I got summoned to see her.

St Peter's and Sister Philomena were probably my first experience of a phenomenon that became very apparent to me as I went through later life. It's a thing that I've noticed about Christians: they know an awful lot about Hell but they can't tell you a square inch of Heaven. If you ask them about Heaven, you get some messy answer about it being a place where you sing God's praises all day. It doesn't sound like a place I much want to go, frankly. But given just how much they knew about it, I figured the nuns at St Peter's must have been taken on a guided tour of Hell.

Florence and I would be sent off to Mass every Sunday. It wasnae too bad. The priest at St Peter's Church would be in his amice, alb, girdle, maniple and stole and would conduct the services in Latin. We had a missal to guide us through Mass. The page was split down the middle with the Latin on the left and the English translation on the right so you could follow what the priest was saying and recite the answers. I liked being picked to go around with the plate but I had more fun showing Florence how to yawn and set off everybody else. We would see it going along our pew, then right around the church.

When I was in the Cubs, I got chosen to be an altar boy, but this was not to be a great success. The other lads and I got to the sacristy and we all wanted to be the guy who holds the thurible with the incense in it and swings it around during the service so that all the incense puffs out. We all made a grab for the thing as soon as we saw it hanging up and a huge rammy broke out in the sacristy, with a few fists flying. The priest flung me and another boy out and that was the end of my altar boy career.

When I was eight or so I also got conscripted into a purportedly very devout band of youth called the Children of Mary. We used to knock on people's doors and go in their homes to say the rosary with them. We were like the kiddie wing of what Scots call the Holy Willies, after the great Robert Burns poem 'Holy Willie's Prayer' about the kind of humourless religious maniacs that anybody sane avoids like the plague. When people opened the door to us tiny Holy Willies, you could see the thought bubble over their heads: *Oh, fuck!* They might turn us away with an excuse – 'My parents aren't here', 'We're in the middle of dinner' – but people were afeart of the Church in those days, so more often than not we'd be let in.

We would have a little statue of the Lady of Lourdes in a

shoebox with us and we would put it on the mantelpiece in their front room and all kneel on the floor to say the rosary. Our hosts would be well pissed off because they were waiting to watch *Coronation Street*. We kids would say the first half of the Lord's Prayer:

> *Our father who art in heaven*
> *Hallowed be thy name.*
> *Thy kingdom come, thy will be done*
> *On earth as it is in heaven.*

Then our hosts would reply – as quickly as they could, because they wanted to get rid of us pious little fuckers and watch *Corrie*:

> *Give us this day our daily bread*
> *And forgive us our trespasses*
> *As we forgive those who trespass against us.*
> *Lead us not into temptation*
> *But deliver us from evil*
> *Forthineisthekingdomthepowerandthegloryforeverandeveramen.*

Then it was our turn again, as we got to the Hail Marys:

> *Hail Mary, full of grace*
> *The Lord is with thee.*
> *Blessed are thou amongst women*
> *And blessed is the fruit of thy womb, Jesus.*

At this point the theme from *Coronation Street* would come wafting through next door's wall – '*Da, da da da-da-da!*' – and the people kneeling around us would gabble:

HolyMaryMotherofGodprayforussinnersnowandatthehourofour-deathAmen.

We'd be back in the street with our virgin mother in a shoebox thirty seconds later, on our way to torment our next poor victims.

When my family moved to Drumchapel the church services we went to took a turn for the worse. St Peter's in Partick had been an ancient old church where my grandparents had got married and the sermons were all about the usual stuff: the Bible, and good and evil. When we got to Drumchapel there was no church at first, and when they quickly knocked one up, St Pius X, it smelled of cement and paint. The sermons consisted of the priest, Father Cassidy, haranguing us from the pulpit for money every week: '*We need money to build this church and pay for it!*' It was extremely fucking boring.

As a kid I went along with saying my prayers and going to Mass and carting the Virgin Mary around the tenements in a shoebox because, like any kid, I didn't know any better. It was just *how things were* and part of my everyday life. I sang the hymns at school, and I really liked some of them: 'For Those in Peril on the Sea' is still one of my favourite songs. The religious education lessons each morning were dull, though. If I tried to ask the teacher a question in Bible studies – 'If Adam and Eve were the only people on Earth, where did Cain and Abel's wives come from?' or 'Did Jesus have any brothers or sisters?' – I got ignored or, on a bad day, whacked with the tawse, so I stopped doing that.

It was only as I got older, and could start to think for myself, that I realised the depth of the discrimination against Catholics that was all around me. It began to feel like it was *them and us*. There was this phrase that I would hear all the time, that people would tell us to our faces: *'This is a Protestant country.'* I could never understand that. I used to ask people, 'What do you mean by that? That I have fewer rights than you?' Nobody could really explain it to me. It just gave me this sort of second-best feeling: that I wasn't really welcome here. It angered me. It was the same rejection my parents' generation had felt – and, of course, that had made them cling to their Catholic faith all the more.

When I started in the shipyard, on my very first day working in the stores, Willie Bain took me up to meet the glue-maker, Tam. Tam was a very important guy in Stephen's for two reasons: he made the glue for all the joiners in the yard, and also his oven had hotplates, and if he liked you, he might let you heat your lunchtime pie up on them. Willie took me up and called the glue-maker over.

'Eh, Tam, I've got a new boy for ye.'

'Oh, aye?' said Tam, and wandered over from his glue pots to have a look at me. He stared at me, walked around to the side to have a go from another angle, and then told Willie, 'Turn him half around.' Tam had a good peer at me from all four sides, squinted a bit, nodded to himself, and said: 'Catholic!'

On our way back to the stores, Willie told me he had never known Tam to be wrong. It was funny, but it also underlined the bigotry and prejudice that underpinned everyday life. Once I had a job interview at an iron-and-steel-tube manufacturer in Ruther-glen. There was only one other applicant: a Protestant guy who was too pissed to fill out his application form properly. I had to help him. A key question asked which school we had been to. The Prot-estant guy got the job. I wasnae surprised.*

Yet as I moved through my teens, it was experiences in the shipyard that helped me to realise that religion wasn't for me. When I was an apprentice welder, I was staggered to find that some welders didn't like being a welder, or didn't like their wives, or didn't like where they lived, or didn't like Catholics, or didn't like Protestants . . . their whole lives seemed to be dominated by *things that they didnae like*. Even at that age, I knew I wanted my life to be

---

* Scottish Presbyterianism can reach into all areas of the country's life. D. C. Thomson, the Dundee publishers of the *Sunday Post*, *The People's Friend*, the *Beano* and the *Dandy*, has always been a famously religious, puritanical organ-isation. Back in the Sixties, I was playing in Broughty Ferry and I got asked if I wanted to meet Dudley D. Watkins, who drew the *Oor Wullie* and *The Broons* cartoon strips. I was not a fan of the strips but he is a legendary figure in Scotland, so I said that I'd love to meet him. This got passed on to him, but a message came back to me: 'Dudley wants to know if you are born again?' I sent word back that, no, I was very much not born again. This didn't best please Dudley: 'Well, I'm not interested in meeting *him*, then!'

controlled by things that I liked. I've kept that philosophy right through until today.

There was no blinding flash on the road to Damascus but I started thinking about all the religious stories I had been force-fed, all the way through from primary school. I began to question everything – *Jesus came from a virgin birth?* Eh? What was *that* all about? And the Blessed Trinity of the Father, the Son and the Holy Ghost – what the fuck was all that? What, God is His own father? So why does He keep saying He gave us His own son, if it was Himself all along? I came to realise, *This is all nonsense, I don't believe it*, and I just slid out of it. I left it behind.

It felt like a relief, an escape, but at the time my father, particularly, was really troubled by the fact that I had rejected religion. I think an awful lot of people of his generation went to church and maybe didn't believe those fairy stories any more than me. They were in the habit of going and it was part of their routine and their life. It helped to explain their lives to them and it gave them a reason for existing and going to work and . . . being miserable. I just knew now, for sure, that it wasn't for me.

Of course, when I left the shipyard and moved into the world of folk clubs, and left-wing politics, and turned into a peace-and-free-love hippy, I became even more of a debauched heathen. I guess this was probably never more spectacularly illustrated than the night that I smoked the Bible.

It was in the Humblebums days, and Gerry and I had just played a gig in some remote corner of the Highlands up near John O'Groats.

We used to play these little folk clubs and the promoter would say the fee would be x amount of money plus accommodation. This normally meant a couch or the floor. So, Gerry and I were sharing a room in this guy's house, very drunk, and although I never really got on with hashish, I had this Pakistani black on me, the kind that is so strong that after you smoke it you find yourself walking under low traffic bridges and ducking. Our problem was that we had no papers – or skins, as we cool cats used to call them back then. Now, John O'Groats and the Scottish Highlands were not in the vanguard of the hippy revolution. If you asked somebody for a skin, they'd probably hand you a sheepskin. But I had a bright idea.

'I saw a prison movie once where they were smoking the Bible,' I told Gerry. 'It looked like a page of the Bible makes reasonable cigarette paper. I'll go up to the guy's bedroom and see if he is still awake and ask him if he has a Bible.'

I staggered off to find the promoter's bedroom and found him sitting on his bed, reading a book. He was as pissed as I was but I remember that he was trying to read a book about how to recognise war planes by their silhouettes. For some reason, that was his bedtime reading of choice that particular night.

'Excuse me, you wouldn't happen to have a Bible, would you?' I asked him.

'Aye, I've got a Bible,' he said. 'Do you want it?'

'I just want a couple of pages.'

'Sure, do you want any particular pages?'

I told him that I wasnae bothered, so he ripped out a few pages from his Bible and gave them to me, and I took them back down to Gerry so we could get smoking. I didn't notice which chapter of the Bible the pages had come from but once that Pakistani black was inside us, I'm pretty sure that it was Revelation.

When I was at St Peter's Primary School I had been told that God was dead and it was all my fault; now I had killed him again, in that I had banished him from my life. I wasn't filled with any burning hatred towards religion, though, or all the nonsense I'd been taught in its name over the years. I thought it was daft and I wanted nothing to do with it, but I was more inclined to see the funny side of some of its stories, and when I started my comedy career that led me to the Last Supper and Crucifixion on Gallowgate. I didn't perform it to offend anybody or to cause an outrage. I did it because I thought it was funny, but the religious backlash to the Last Supper routine was immense. The Scottish newspapers went mental about it and a lot of senior Church people declared how dreadful it was and condemned it as sacrilegious. A couple of progressive priests defended me and told the papers that they liked it and they even thought it might help some people to relate to religion, but they were very much the exception. Most Church people hated it and evangelist preachers began to picket and demonstrate outside of my shows.

I hadn't tried to pick a fight with religion but I found myself right in the middle of one. The most persistent of the evangelists who used to follow me around was a guy called Pastor Jack Glass, who wasn't much older than me. He used to turn up outside my concerts with followers and they would sing hymns. I noticed that none of them seemed to blink very much. Pastor Glass followed me all the way to shows in Wales. He used to carry three nails and whenever he saw me outside a show, he would yell, 'Crucify Christ again!' He used to have a bag of coins, thirty pieces of silver, and once he hit me right in the forehead with it. The coins went flying all over the place.

On the first night of my first Australian tour, in Brisbane in 1976, a bunch of Scottish religious nuts in the audience yelled anti-Catholic abuse at me and sang Rangers songs. It was so bad that I had to stop the show and beat a retreat off the stage. I got seriously worried – was this how things were going to be for me all the time from now on? Luckily, the rest of the Aussie tour was OK, the scandal media moved on to their next victim, and the outrage over the Last Supper died down (apart from the dogged Pastor Glass, who was still waving his three nails at me). But it got pretty hairy for a while.

I was baffled at the time as to why the Church was up in such high dudgeon against one guy telling a funny story. But now I look back at it all, more than forty years on, I think the Last Supper was a good stand for me to make. If the Church, with its many millions, was scared of me, it must have been in deep trouble. I am still proud that I took them on and, in a funny way, I beat them.

Once I had seen through the nonsense about virgin births and Jesus dying for our sins, I relaxed about the whole issue of religion.

It didn't bug me. It just became an irrelevance to my life that I didn't need to bother about. Yet the Church and the sectarian divide continued to shape so many people's lives. There is still a deep-seated religious angst in Scotland that shows few signs of abating, and nowhere does that tension manifest itself more strongly than in the Celtic/Rangers obsession.

When my father started taking me to Celtic in the Fifties I absolutely loved it. I idolised the players, and football has given me some of the best memories of my life. I'll never forget some of the Scottish Cup Finals with 110,000 people in Hampden Park. You'd see people who had fainted being passed bodily over the heads of the fans like a rock star in an audience. The crowds all had wooden rattles and the noise the fans made was incredible. When I was leaving at the end, squashed between all the adults, I could lift my feet and levitate my way out of the ground. It was extraordinary.

Celtic fans used to sing hymns on the terraces during the matches:

> *Hail glorious St Patrick, dear saint of our isle*
> *On us thy poor children bestow a sweet smile.*
> *And though thou art high in thy mansions above*
> *On Erin's green valley look down in thy love.*

It was remarkable. You would get these tens of thousands of people singing: *'On Erin's green valley, on Erin's green valley . . .'* It was like a Welsh rugby match atmosphere. Rangers fans didn't do anything like that. They used to just sing, *'Follow, follow, we will follow Rangers . . .'*

I loved Celtic and it was great when we won, which we usually did, but I was never too bothered if we lost. It didn't eat me up. And I never got into the thing of hating Rangers, even though they were obviously our big rivals. It never made sense to me. My attitude was a long way from being typical, though. There was only one Rangers supporter in my Catholic secondary school and he was as brave as Tarzan. He used to wear his Rangers scarf over his green blazer. He endured relentless abuse every day: 'Boo! Get that off, ye bastard!' In the winter he would be submerged under hails of snowballs. But he persevered.

There was an even more extreme case in the shipyard when one of the apprentice welders changed his allegiance overnight from being a Celtic supporter to a rabid Rangers fan. That was a thing that just *never* happened. He never said why he did it and he got a seriously hard time but he stood his ground, which I thought was admirable. But the biggest diehard Rangers fan in the shipyard was a caulker called Big Sammy. When I was still an apprentice, I called him a bluenose bastard one day and ran off, but he chased after me and caught me. The carpenters and painters in the yard used to line off the deck with French chalk, to mark where the bulkheads were going to lie, and they would paint a little right angle of blue paint. Sammy grabbed me, held me down on the deck, grabbed the paint and painted my nose blue.

I loved football, and rivalry and banter with Rangers fans could be great, but the *hatred* that it seemed to engender in many people baffled me. I have known people right through my life, from when I was in the shipyards and from just being around Glasgow, who went to Rangers matches and yelled abuse at the opposition all through the game; *'You fucking Catholic bastards! You Fenian wankers!'* Then after the match they came back out through the gates, went home and were nothing at all like that in their normal day-to-day lives. It was as if it was a hobby for them: *bigotry as a hobby.*

The sectarian prejudice always seemed stronger within Rangers than Celtic to me. Celtic has never been an anti-Protestant club. The legendary Celtic team that beat Inter Milan to win the European Cup in 1967 had seven Protestant players and four Catholics, and a Protestant manager, Jock Stein.* Rangers, however, always were a 100 per cent Protestant club. They started as a Presbyterian rowing club in the Gare Loch in 1872 and when they became a football club, the Presbyterian thing stuck right up until the Seventies. Even the guy selling the pies would be a Protestant.

It was when Graham Souness became their manager in the Eighties that he changed things by signing Catholic players such as Mo Johnston. It was a very brave move by him. Some Rangers fans were disgusted and stopped going to matches, saying they would

---

* Jock was a massive hero to me and it was such a thrill when I got to know him. He said a funny thing to me once. Jock always had a problem with his weight, even when he was a player, while I was a skinny bugger back then. Jock told me one day: 'Connolly, you're built like the gable end of a pound note!'

never come back. Most of them eventually inched their way back, though. They couldn't keep away.* Everything has changed nowadays and Rangers have Italian and Spanish players playing for them, who are obviously Catholic. Even so, the club still discourage them from making the sign of the cross and blessing themselves as they walk on the pitch, as so many players do.

There have always been Rangers pubs and Celtic pubs dotted around Glasgow and Scotland. Originally it just used to mean that they were the pubs that the supporters' coaches would leave from to go to the matches. Nowadays there are Celtic pubs that only Celtic supporters go to and Rangers fans are not welcome, and Rangers pubs that are the opposite. It's not all quite as evil as it sounds – generally it tends to be because the regulars just want to talk about their own team. But there is a famous Rangers pub in Kilwinning, in Ayrshire, where you are not allowed in if you are wearing anything green.

It would be lovely to think, in 2018, that the hatred between Rangers and Celtic, between Protestant and Catholic, had all evaporated into the ether. But I think it is still there and it holds Scotland back as a nation. There was a movement against it a few years ago, a kind of anti-bigotry movement, but it seems to have

---

* Twenty years ago, Rangers had Paul Gascoigne playing for them and he mimed playing the flute when he scored a goal, as if he was on an Orange march. That was a funny one and it made me laugh, partly because Gazza is a crazy man but also because he got his hands all wrong. Your hands don't both face the same way when you play the flute.

fizzled out and it didn't really come to anything. The Scottish press don't help; they always fan the rivalry and the Catholic/Protestant divide until people aren't sure where the truth lies.

If you read the newspapers, only Celtic and Rangers exist in Scotland. For example, Rangers have just got a new manager, Steven Gerrard from Liverpool, and the only question the papers are asking is: 'Will Steven Gerrard have the beating of Celtic?' They don't say anything about Aberdeen, who came second in the league last year, ahead of Rangers. There are a million people in Glasgow and they don't all support either Celtic or Rangers. Some of them support Partick Thistle, or Bayern Munich, or just don't give a toss about football. The media don't speak about these people, as if they don't exist.

Celtic kindly gave me a seat for life a while ago (along with Rod Stewart) and I still go to every game I can when I'm in Scotland. I went to the Cup Final this year and it was a boring game but we won. We have been doing great lately – *the Double Treble, and don't you forget it!* Rangers have been in trouble, though, having to make their way back up through the leagues after financial problems. I would like them to get better again because a good Rangers improves Celtic – as does a good Hibs or a good Hearts or a good Aberdeen. In truth, the Celtic/Rangers rivalry doesn't matter – I actually wish Celtic could play in the English Premier League, the best league in the world.

In football and in Scotland, sectarian hatred belongs in the past and I'd like to think that it is not as bad as it was. Then, sometimes,

I wonder if I am deluding myself and being too hopeful. Only last season, Neil Lennon, who used to be the Celtic manager and is now the manager of Hibs, ran on the pitch and celebrated when his team scored a fifth goal, making it Hibs 5, Rangers 5. He got punished by the Scottish FA for going over the top, but he explained why he had done it: 'The Rangers supporters were calling me a Fenian bastard all match long!' We still have a long way to go. I don't understand how we're ever going to get rid of the bigotry – it seems bottomless. I'm just grateful that I have always got along well with Glaswegians as a whole, all of them.

Along with the *dreich* weather, the dominance of religion has always been a big factor behind the pessimism of character that has made the Scots infamous. Scottish people in the generations up to and including mine feared the Church and were very devout. I have seen that changing in my lifetime. Young people nowadays generally don't give a toss about religion.

The Church has held Scotland back for too many years and, even today, religion can make people do the strangest things. I recently went up to the Isle of Lewis to meet a lovely artist named Moira Maclean, who creates art installations using old Gaelic Bibles. Moira told me that very few people in the Hebrides are worshipping in Gaelic any more but some of the older people don't know what to do with their old Bibles because they don't dare throw them away – it feels wrong, and sinful, to them. So, a man digs a hole in the local graveyard and they bury the Bibles in there. They lay them to rest.

If I am honest, I find Christianity a bit of a pain in the arse, but even though I'm an atheist, I worry about those who campaign against religion too devoutly – they seem to have a wee bit too much religious fervour themselves. I know that many people get a lot of strength from their faith and I respect that. Ultimately, for me, *religion is just there*, a strange and inexplicable part of life. The sectarian divide still exists, and Glasgow still has its big Orange march each year, which finishes up on Glasgow Green. But I think in recent years more and more people are becoming intolerant of *that stuff* – they are swinging against it and rejecting it. It's the same as in Ireland, which this year turned on the Catholic Church for the first time ever with the big vote in favour of legalising abortion: people in Scotland are finally making their big decisions *based on healthier things*. And long may it continue.

'We'll Never Be That Boy Again' . . . A Conversation on Friendship

I can't remember exactly how I first met Peter McDougall. He's been an essential part of my life since . . . forever. He grew up in Greenock and was in the shipyards, like me, as a youth. Then he moved down to London to become a house painter and impressed the actor and Oscar-winning screenwriter Colin Welland, whose house he was painting, with his intelligence and storytelling. Colin advised Peter to write a play and the upshot was *Just Another Saturday*, about Peter's experiences of going on Orange marches as a lad. It got made for the BBC as a *Play for Today* in 1975 – I was in it – and it won awards and set

I've known Peter since . . . forever

Peter on his way to becoming one of Scotland's great working-class writers and dramatists.

I went on to do two or three more plays for Peter and he encouraged me to write as well. I'd been fiddling around just doing little bits and pieces and Peter said, 'No, sit down and write something, finish it and send it to me.' Then he told me to get things like *An' Me Wi' A Bad Leg* staged, which I wrote in 1976. I don't do anything like that any more but way back in the day I had a play put on in the official Edinburgh Festival and two in the Fringe, and that was largely down to Peter and his encouragement.

Peter comes from the same background as me and, like me, he never forgets that to have launched from working-class Glasgow and the shipyards into these other, airy-fairy heights – and to be applauded by the great and the good in the way that we have been – is a fine thing. He is a splendid Scottish writer and a complete curmudgeon. Even when we live thousands of miles apart, as we do now, he remains one of my very closest friends. I met up with him in the Òran Mór bar and theatre near his home in the West End of Glasgow this summer, and we talked about how we are both falling to fucking bits.

Me: You're looking great.

Peter: I should do. I was up at eight o'clock this morning to meet you at three this afternoon. You look good, too.

Me: I'm hanging in there. Taking my medicine.

Peter: Oh, me and all.

Me: I have to take them three or four times a day.

Peter: It's a pain in the fucking arse, isn't it?

Me: Especially this fucking Parkinson's – it's not going to
           go away.

Peter: I've got nothing like that, but I had Legionnaires' disease. It
           took me six months to learn to walk again. Then when I was
           recovering from that, I had a fucking stroke. I can't walk very
           well now but that's OK. I've been drunk most of my life, so
           people just think, *Ah, that cunt's drunk again.*

Me: Aye, you're lucky there.

Peter: I wear suits now to cover all my infirmities. I've always been a
           tart, but now I dress in spotless three-piece suits every day,
           even when I'm only going to Tesco. I think I'm saying, *This is*
           the man I used to be, because my head's not there. I've got a
           thing called aphasia, and I just go missing. I'm getting fucking
           glimpses of dementia. It's not just forgetting where you're
           going, I forget where I put the fridge.

Me: As we Scots say, you're a bit wandert.*

Peter: It never ends. I had an operation to have a kidney stone out.
           I came to wrapped in tinfoil, with an eight-person trauma
           team around me at three in the morning. It turned out I had
           fucking sepsis.

Me: You had sepsis? You're lucky you're here at all.

Peter: I know. I thought I'd hang on for you.

---

* An old Scots word meaning confused; bewildered; at a loss.

Me: Aye. I often find myself wanting to say to people, *Actually, I'm still in here. I've got symptoms, but I still live in here.* I have trouble getting out of bed. I have to do a sort of see-saw move to get my legs out, and then swing my body out.

Peter: I have to go to the clinic in Partick every week for my Warfarin for my heart. It always reminds me of how we used to put it down in the shipyards to kill rats.

Me: Aye, we used it as rat poison. Is that the same clinic we used to go to as kids for the dentist?

Peter: Aye, it is.

Me: It was terrifying. They used to give us gas.

Peter: I remember that. The short-term memory goes but there is so much I remember about me and you.

Me: Aye, back in the day I used to just lift a phone and you were there. We had a funny thing going.

Peter: I remember the first time you took me to your home and I met your family. There was damp washing on the pulley and the second that I saw it, I knew you and I had the same background.

Me: We always had the pulley with the washing drying in the kitchen.

Peter: I remember the smell, especially when it was slightly damp. And I remember you coming to see me in Greenock, in the days you used to drink. We were standing on a train and two hardmen got on, both in starched denim jeans and jacket. You said, *'That's a Greenock uniform, and the important thing is, it has to be spotless.'*

Me: Ha! I remember that.

Peter: Do you remember that amazing brown leather jerkin I bought in New York?

Me: I do. My guinea pig ate a hole in it.

Peter: I was sleeping on your couch, and I woke up, and the bugger's on its hind legs, eating my fucking jerkin.

Me: That was Vinnie, my guinea pig.

Peter: Oh, I thought he was a rabbit. My memory lets me down. I loved that jacket. It had a Teamsters Union 1959 badge on it.

Me: Aye, it was an *On the Waterfront* jacket.

Peter: And a fucking guinea pig ate it in Highland Road! I took it to a seamstress and she cut out the shape of a buffalo and stitched it on to cover the hole.

Me: How's your writing going lately?

Peter: I'm writing a play – is it my tenth? But the thing is, I don't care now whether they get made or not. It doesnae matter. I write poetry and bits like that. Working with you, getting the pieces out that we did back in the day, they were . . . seminal. People still talk to me about *The Elephants' Graveyard** and I still think

---

* *The Elephants' Graveyard* was another McDougall *Play for Today* in 1976 in which I played an unemployed hardman with a secret. It was full of brilliant lines: '*You get neither chance nor choice. You leave school and go straight to work without even thinking about it. Then you get married without even knowing about it. Then you spend the rest of your days using both as an excuse for never having done anything with your life.*'

the way you played the bank robber was fucking unbelievable. You gave it an amazing depth.

Me: That was down to your words.

Peter: No, it wasnae that. People like to pigeonhole, and when I tell them you played a gangster and you played it well, they just think it was because you have a natural hardness as a Glaswegian. But that's wrong.

Me: Aye, a lot of people think if you have a working-class background, you're endowed with some kind of hardman vibe. It's bullshit.

Peter: I remember the night before we started filming *The Elephants' Graveyard*, you came to me all niggly and said, 'I cannae learn all that tonight!' I said, 'You're not fucking learning the whole thing!'

Me: Aye, I remember that. I thought I had to learn everything. *Play for Today* was an important series. It put British writers in the spotlight.

Peter: In those days writers were important, before directors took over. The fucking arrogance and the sense of entitlement they have, and they couldnae direct traffic.

Me: They couldnae direct the Clyde past Dumbarton Rock.

Peter: What did we used to say in the shipyard? *'Call yourself a fucking electrician, you couldn't wire a hutch.'*

Me: *'You couldnae get juice out of a Jaffa.'*

Peter: *'You couldnae tack the high road.'*

Me: *'You couldnae plate soup.'*

Peter: Look, I want to tell you something. I wrote a speech for you
for that National Television Award you got a while back but
I never gave it. I'm not sure if I'm going to read it to you now.

Me: Read it if you want to and don't if you don't.

Peter: Aye, I will read it [*produces paper and reads*]:

You get kind of fed up and can become easily inured to the use of the word 'genius'. It's nearly as irritating as 'awesome'. Especially when it's applied to a football player who can do a scissors kick, or a tennis player who can whack a ball into a net at 160 miles an hour. Good for them, but genius? My arse. But Billy Connolly is. He's a man unto himself. Unique. His intelligence, perspicacity, and his wonderful ability to mime his very language produces performances that are at times mesmeric.

Years ago, as only a part of a story, he told me about a wee wean out and about with his ma, in Partick, holding her hand. He was spitting up in the air, and she said, 'What are you doing?' and he said, 'I'm raining on myself.' The insightfulness of that observation can still have me, and probably lots of men, waking in the night longing for the loss of that spitting boy. Because Mr Connolly's images and words live with you long after and can bring a smile to your face and a chuckle to your throat when you least expect it, like when you're sitting in a doctor's waiting room. Billy Connolly is not just talented, he is gifted, and he is our gift. It is my pleasure that he and I have been friends for nigh on fifty years. But more importantly, perhaps, over those years it's

been my privilege, and yours, to have been allowed the glimpses
that he gives of his genius.

Me: Oh, that's very kind of you.

Peter: The thing about the spitting boy . . . what you were talking
        about there, without possibly knowing it yourself, was the fact
        that *we'll never be that boy again.*

Me: I'd forgotten all about that. It's come back to me like an old
        friend. They don't come easy, those lines.

Peter: Of course not. Everybody thinks that stuff just happens and
        comes out. It disnae. It comes from the fucking depths of . . .
        not even knowing yourself where it comes from.

Me: Yesterday I was thinking about the Upper Clyde shipbuilders:
        Jimmy Reid and all the guys. It was a fucking astonishing time.

Peter: It was. He was a good man, Jimmy.

Me: He was a very good man, an honourable man. None of your
        clapperboard shite there. And there were shipyard guys like
        Willie McInnes, who wasn't as erudite but when he spoke he
        was just as strong and true.

Peter: Jimmy was a lovely man. The last time I saw him was at your
        party. That fire, that enthusiasm . . .

Me: He made the men believe in themselves. He didn't
        brainwash them. He woke them up as to what they
        actually were.

Peter: Of course, one of the things that mattered was getting them
        not to drink.

Me: *Nae bevvying.*

Peter: *Nae bevvying.* But we were thrown into the welding, weren't we, you and me? We were fifteen . . . you tell people now and they think you're talking about Dickensian days.

Me: When you see films of it, it looks like Dickensian days.

Peter: You see a fifteen-year-old boy today and you think, *I was out grafting at your age.* You say it to your own weans.

Me: My grandson just had his sixteenth birthday. I said, 'I was an apprentice on the Clyde when I was your age.'

Peter: You'd get up in the morning, out on the schemes, in the snow, and it was like a Lowry snowscape with these wee men all running for buses. Sometimes your bus couldnae make it up the hill and you'd be late. Then you couldnae get any time off work.

Me: The bus windows would be all misted up on the inside and you'd make a wee hole with the end of your finger to see out. You didnae want to make your whole hand cold.

Peter: It was fucking freezing. People don't understand how cold it was. I worked on the hunter-killer submarines so I'd go down a ladder on that conning tower and I felt that my skin was going to snap with the cold and stick to the metal ladder. I would be in there all day. I didnae see daylight. One of my torments was there was a big, big man that wandered about, up and down the submarine passageway. He had a fucking crucifix tattooed on his chest, and he used to stare at me because he knew I was in the Orange Lodge.

A CONVERSATION ON FRIENDSHIP
· · · · · · · · ·

Me: Oh my God.

Peter: That was weird, that I was so young and going on Orange marches. It was just kind of *something to do,* you looked forward to it because your life was so depressing. And that's what I wrote about in *Just Another Saturday.** I didn't know anybody in the parades that actually hated Catholics, although that was what the songs were about and what people were shouting. It was just a day out. You'd get your drink and fall about.

Me: The other week I saw a wee Orange band and it was the Partick guys, the Partick Truth Defenders. They were marching past the Kelvin Hall and they were playing 'Any Dream Will Do' from *Joseph and the Amazing Technicolor Dreamcoat*: '*I close my eyes, do-do-do-do-do . . .*' I thought that just about summed it up.

Peter: Aye, they'll play anything now! *The Sound of Music.* What happened to 'The Sash' and 'Derry's Walls'?

Me: They've gone glam. They'll play anything that will go down well. I'd like to think it's a sign that bigotry is dying out – but it's still around. A lot of people don't realise the depth of it in this country.

---

* *Just Another Saturday* was originally rejected by the BBC because of its sensitive subject matter of Orange marches. When they then made it for *Play for Today*, filming was halted for a year after the Glasgow Chief of Police warned that it would lead to 'bloodshed in the streets in the making and the showing'.

Peter: No. There was a very unpleasant thing when Celtic played
         Rangers a while back. A Rangers player was taking a corner
         and he was a Peruvian, I think. A Celtic supporter flung a
         cigarette lighter at him. Celtic were four nothing up at the
         time, so why would he do that? But he wasnae flinging it at the
         guy – he was flinging it at the shirt. He was flinging it at 200
         years of history and badness.

Me: Christ. It just never lets up.

Peter: It doesnae. It slowly gets better but it takes a really long time.
         But that stuff was all part and parcel of our time in the
         shipyards, wasn't it?

Me: Aye. I still sometimes think back to when we used to come out
         of the gates at night, when all those thousands of men poured
         onto the street – where did they all go?

Peter: I don't know. *They're deid.* My grandfather was a boilermaker.
         He retired at sixty-five: you had to, in those days. Every day
         after he retired he stood at that gate and watched guys
         running out, hoping to see somebody he knew, because he
         had nothing else to do. They didn't have allotments or
         anything like that then.

Me: I was talking about this the other day . . . when the guys
         retired they'd get a wallet of notes and a watch. They'd come
         back and see you a few times . . . and they'd last for eighteen
         months if they were lucky before they died.

Peter: Aye. *They were off.* I was at my younger brother John's funeral
         yesterday.

Me: Oh, no. What happened to him?

Peter: He died on his sixtieth birthday. And I'm proud to say that he uttered a line of mine as he went.

Me: You're kidding me?

Peter: No. His wife told me that he was lying there in pain, his kidney had failed, and he just said, *'Argh, I'm fed up with this. That's me away now.'*

Me: *That's me away now.*

Peter: That's what I wrote. A guy tells his wife, *'Tell the doctor, that's me away now.'* And she shouts out, *'Doctor, that's him away now.'* And he's off.

Me: That's a proud way to go. What was wrong with John?

Peter: He had diabetes. But I'll tell you a funny story about him. You know he was a carpenter. Well, one time there were some people coming up to see me from London to talk about films. I thought I'd take them to Inverkip Marina, because they don't see the sea in London. We went down there and walked into a restaurant and the guy behind the bar said, 'Are you Peter McDougall?' I said, 'Aye', and reached into my pocket for a pen to sign him an autograph. But it wasnae that he wanted. He said, 'See that fucking brother, John, of yours? Tell him to get his fucking terrible tools out of here. They've been lying here that long, I'm going to put them into the *Antiques Roadshow*.' Because John would just fuck off and leave his tools everywhere. He never finished a kitchen in his life.

Me: Ha! Was the funeral in Greenock?

Peter: Aye. Greenock reminds me now of the first time you go to America, when you drive into a town and all you pass is malls and McDonald's and you think, *This isnae a town.* It's like that now.

Me: Really? It's still got a shipyard, hasn't it?

Peter: No. There's just the Ferguson in Port Glasgow.

Me: Oh aye, the one with the castle in it.*

Peter: Do you remember the story I told you about that, years ago? There was a Labour councillor in Greenock who was always fucking drunk, and he was pissed and asleep in a council meeting about Ferguson and the rights to the castle. He woke up, and said, *'Who the fuck was daft enough to build a castle in the middle of a shipyard anyway?'*

Me: I remember. Did the funeral have a good turnout?

Peter: Aye, but I'd rather not have gone if I could get away with it. Every fucking funeral you go to takes you a step nearer your end, and I'm not ready for that yet.

Me: Nor me.

Peter: You glimpse your own frailty, and sometimes you even think, *I wish I had fucking religion.* I've got a line in the play I'm writing: *'I've developed a limp from carrying coffins.'* And then it's the whole thing of going back to Greenock. Everyone that

---

* Newark Castle was built on the Clyde in 1478 but when the river became a shipbuilding centre at the end of the nineteenth century it found itself surrounded by shipyards.

I knew in Greenock is dead now, but I still go there and look for spiritual significance because I come from there.

Me: The same thing happens every time I come back to Glasgow. I see all the things that I like but they're not anywhere I could cling to.

Peter: There's that wonderful line: *'To go back to where you come from is to know it for the first time.'* There's an umbilical cord that pulls you back. I am still searching for some kind of spark to ignite in me in Greenock, but maybe . . . *there's fuck-all to search for.* You were born there and that's it. But unless you cut that umbilical cord completely you always come back.

Me: Aye. I suppose you and I knew from a young age we were going to go away.

Peter: I remember when I decided to leave the shipyard and go to London. My ma said, 'Son, don't go. That's not for the likes of you.' My ma had never taken a bus to the middle of Greenock, let alone go to London. She knew nothing, it was all in her head, but she was trying to protect me. Your parents say, 'Don't go there, don't move out of your comfort zone,' but it's *their* comfort zone, not yours.

Me: That's right. They know boys who got intelligent at school and went to university; they would come back with a different accent and not fit in any more.

Peter: My ma thought I'd get hurt in the big, wide world and not cope with it because I wasn't of the *class* to cope with people.

Me: Aye, it was all about class. It still is. When I was starting out, the way I was written about in the newspapers here was all to do with class. *'Connolly's language is disgraceful . . .'* and yet people were fucking and blinding in plays and nobody said a word about it.

Peter: You came through at the same time as that Cambridge Footlights crowd. They swore, and it was all, 'Aren't they so frightfully clever?'

Me: Yes. If they swore it was OK.

Peter: Growing up the way we were . . . *you're brought up under a fucking hammer.* You're expected to stay put. Would somebody believe that I write fucking papers on existentialism for the fucking Sorbonne? That I know about fucking Sartre? Of course not, *because I come from Greenock.*

My grandfather used to put me by his knee and sing to me, when I was a wean. The song he used to sing was:

> *There once was an old man called McKnight*
> *He challenged a navvy out to fight.*
> *He hit him in the jaw and he nearly broke it*
> *He didnae know the navvy had a hammer in his pocket*
> *He hit McKnight and he fell.*
> *Where he is we cannot tell.*
> *He's either in heaven or in Hamilton.*

And he'd say 'Hamilton' because you couldnae say 'Hell'. But
you could hit a guy with a hammer.

Me: Now *there's* a thing to learn at your grandfather's knee.

Peter: Aye. You have to laugh. You know, I overheard two women,
not so long ago, talking about my wife, Morag. They didn't
see me nearby. One of them said, 'You must know Morag?
She cares for that wee, fat, baldy man that doesn't
keep well.'

Me: Ha! I had one of those. I was filming where I was brought up in
Partick. The director went for a cigarette and I was being
besieged for autographs next to Kerr's, the wee shop in the
street I used to live in. There were schoolchildren all around
me, I was signing autographs and the director was sitting
having a fag in his car. There were two women outside the car
and he heard one of them say:
'What's going on over there at Kerr's?'
The other one said, 'It's Billy Connolly, he's signing
autographs.'
There was a silence for about a minute and then the first one
sighed and said:
'It's a shame. His father was *such* a nice man.'

Peter: You know, the good thing about us is we know each other so
well that we may not see each other for years, but when we
meet up, it doesnae matter.

Me: It doesnae matter at all.

Peter: By the way, do you know that Colin Beattie, the guy who owns the bar we're sitting in, has had a huge sculpture made of you?

Me: No. Of me?

Peter: Aye. It's a beautiful bronze sculpture of you and Chic Murray. He had it commissioned. You're sitting on one end of a seesaw and Chic Murray is on the other. It's a lovely piece.

Me: That sounds amazing. What is he going to do with it?

Peter: Well, he wants to put it outside the bar here, but Glasgow Council won't let him. They've told him, 'Move it to Edinburgh,' and Colin said, 'Why the fuck would I want to move it to Edinburgh?'

Me: So, where is it now?

Peter: It's standing in a warehouse. It's been there for years.

Me: *Oh, for fuck's sake . . .*

'NEVER EAT MINCE ON A CLAMMY DAY'

I have always loved that there are such contrasts within Scotland and so many extraordinary sights in the country's geography. As a kid, I thought it was fantastic that there was this amazing wilderness right on Glasgow's doorstep. My first exploration away from the grey city came when I was in the Cubs and we would go five miles out of town to Milngavie. Then when I graduated to the Scouts we would go further out into the wilder country. You're so fortunate in Glasgow that you are only twenty miles from Loch Lomond and the Lomond Hills, which is where the wilderness truly starts.

The Scouts were my real introduction to the Scottish countryside. We would go to Scout camp in a place called Auchengillan and spend the weekend tying knots and putting up tents and taking them down again. We'd sing songs around a campfire about riding along on the crest of a wave and I'd see mountains and rolling hills and rivers and wild goats and deer. It felt like a different planet from the Glasgow tenements and it had a profound effect on me. It gave me a love of the wild Scottish country that has never left me.

As a boy I often used to cycle up to Loch Lomond. You would smell people brewing up at the side of the road and pull over and share their tea with them. There were these spots called drum-ups at the side of the loch, at the back of the beach, and they were stop-offs for drinking tea. I had a tea-can, which was a split can with tea at one end and sugar at the other, and I would hide it in a crack in the wall there. I would get water out of the loch, light a wee fire, pull my tea-can out of its hidey-hole, put a little branch in to catch the weird floaty stuff, and make a cup of tea. It was great to smell a drum-up coming up as you were cycling along. It was such a joy.

Years later, when I started making a few bob from comedy, I bought myself a Flying Scot racing bike. Its frame was hand-built by Rattray's of Alexandra Parade in Glasgow. It was a wee bit too big for me but it was the only one they had at the time and I bought it anyway because I wanted it so much. They sandblasted the words 'The Big Yin' into the crossbar for me. I just loved that bike. I cycled up and down the land on it – from Glasgow to John O'Groats, and all over Loch Lomond and Helensburgh. I gave it away as a present to a production assistant on a West End play I was in many years ago. I have no idea what he did with it, but when I was in Scotland this year I was reunited with my old Flying Scot after fifty years apart and it was very moving. It felt like seeing an old friend again.

My other main great childhood experiences of Scotland outside of Glasgow came each July, when my father took Florence and me on holiday to Rothesay on the Isle of Bute. In the second fortnight in July, the factories would shut down and Glasgow would just empty out as everybody went on holiday down the Clyde. They used to call it the Glasgow Fair holidays. The whole city would have two weeks off and go away, and when we came back from our holidays it would be Paisley's turn.

It was all such an amazing, exciting ritual. We would get the train out of Glasgow Central and it would be jammed with hundreds of people and their suitcases, and children running around, laughing and shouting. When we arrived at Wemyss Bay station, everybody would spew out of the train on to the platform and march down a concrete walkway to the ferry stop like a huge invading army. It was brilliant to see the Clyde and know we were about to sail across it. My father would be saying, 'C'mon, Billy, keep up!' as he strode along, and Florence and I would get more and more carried away with it all.

A ferry would be sitting waiting with its wooden gangway coming down onto the pier, and we'd all pour on. I would be so excited running up the gangway: *'Woah! Here we go!'* The ferries were these great paddle steamers, and I can remember their names as if it were yesterday: the *Jeanie Deans*. The *Queen Mary II*. The *Caledonia*. The *Duchess of Montrose*. The *Waverley*. The one I remember best is the *Marchioness of Breadalbane*. We always seemed to get that one.

When you got on the ferry, the first thing you would hear

would be the fiddling and the accordions as two guys and a woman sang songs on the boat. They would sing tunes like 'The Song of the Clyde':

> *Oh, the River Clyde, the wonderful Clyde,*
> *The name of it thrills me and fills me with pride*
> *And I'm satisfied, whate'er may betide,*
> *The sweetest of songs is the Song of the Clyde.*

The men would sing the song and the woman would go about the ferry with a velvet bag, looking for donations. There was a lovely innocence about it all: singing songs about your country and going down the Clyde for the Glasgow Fair holiday. Everybody was going away at the same time so you'd see all your school friends running around the boat. You would go down to the ferry's engine room to see the paddle steamer engines, with their great huge pistons rolling away. There was a sweetie shop on board where, if you were lucky, your parents would buy you lemonade.

Your parents would inevitably get talking to someone else's parents on the boat and you would meet their children and play with them, and then see them again on holiday. Every boy and girl would have new sand shoes. There was no such thing as sneakers. If your parents had a few bob, you had white plimsolls. If they were a bit skint, you had weird brown ones. I would be dressed to kill in khaki shorts with a snake belt and a T-shirt. I remember having a snake belt that was tartan elastic. *That* was a bit special.

You would sail down the Clyde and the view on the bank either side was like nothing you were used to in Glasgow. It was all forests and gold-coloured harvest fields, what the Scots call *hairst* fields. There is a lovely bit of Scottish verse about it:

O yellow lie the hairst fields along the banks o' Clyde
They are the bonniest hairst fields that ever was beside.

All we had done was step off a train but we had gone from the world we knew into a completely new one. You would meet people that you knew from Glasgow and you wouldn't recognise them because they had their good clothes on. You were used to seeing them in overalls and flat caps but here they were in smart shirts with sleeves rolled up, striding along with their wife and family. You wouldn't know them and they would have to remind you who they were.

One thing I used to love doing on the ferry was feeding the seagulls – throwing pieces of bread up and seeing the birds catch them in the air. That was an adventure for a city boy. On one holiday trip, when I was about eight, my father had sliced a pear down the middle and given half each to me and Florence. I was just about to eat it when: 'Splat!' A seagull shat right on my half a pear. I was inconsolable – cheated out of my pear! That memory has stayed with me far more strongly than it really should. Another holiday treat was that my father used to buy my sister and me classics comics. I'm sure they don't exist any more but they were exactly what they said they were: comic books of classic works of literature such as *Hamlet*. They should bring them back . . . if they want to bore children shitless again.

When we got to Rothesay we would all pile off the paddle steamer and on to the harbour. In fact, that wee port is the exact spot where I learned to tell the time. There was a clock in the harbour about 200 yards away and my father asked me, 'Billy, what time is it on that clock over there?' I was about nine at the time. I said, 'Well, the big hand is at . . .' and that was as far as I got, because my father clonked me in the ear: 'What, ye cannae tell the time, a boy of your age?' I had to go and learn to tell the time very quickly. I think there should be a plaque there now to mark that momentous spot for future generations of children.

Florence and I used to go to the Children's Corner by the harbour and watch the Punch and Judy show. As I recall it now, Punch and Judy was all about murdering children: *'Kill the baby! Kill the baby! Eat the sausages! Look, there's a crocodile!'* That was the educative message we were being given. A guy called Uncle Phil was the MC and a man called Tony did all the Punch and Judy voices. It was the first time I had ever seen a professional performer and I adored it. I would be sitting crunching on seaside rock, feeling it sucking my fillings out, as little kiddie performers led us in sing-songs. I believe, in later years, the young Lulu and Lena Zavaroni used to perform there. We would sing, 'Ma, He's Making Eyes at Me!' or Al Jolson's: 'Swanee': *'How I love you, how I love you, my dear old Swanee!'* It was the Fifties but we were singing songs from the Twenties. Or we'd all sing the Rothesay Bay song:

At Rothesay Bay, at Rothesay Bay, where the children laugh
   and play
Come to Children's Corner, we'll make your troubles go away
There's lots of fun for everyone at the Punch and Judy show . . .
You can bring your ma and pa and we'll all say ta-ta
At dear old Rothesay Bay . . .

The second fortnight in July is traditionally a pretty rainy time of year — as I've always said, there are two seasons in Scotland: June and Winter — so we'd often be sitting in the pouring rain singing those songs. I have photographs of Flo and me standing on the beach in trench coats and wellies holding buckets and spades in a downpour. Glaswegians of my age have all got those photos.

I never got the hang of using the old box cameras. My father would hand it to me and I'd think, *Oh, shit, I've got to take a picture!* It was a square box with a wee window in the top right-hand corner full of upside-down people. I'd lie and say, 'Looks great!' and randomly press the button: 'Click!' My dad always took two rolls of film on our holiday — one for the first week and one for the second. We would get home and he'd send them off to Ilford to be developed. I used to dread them coming back, because he'd see these photos I'd taken of him standing with Florence, both without heads, and he'd say: 'Billy! Come here . . .'

The pelting rain on holiday didn't stop Florence and me swimming in the sea in our swimming costumes. My costume was a monstrosity that still traumatises me to this day. My aunt had knitted it for me, which meant that it was made of wool and had no elastic. I had to wear a belt with it. It had a wee pocket knitted in it. I wondered for years what I was supposed to keep in there. Maybe four pennies for the telephone in case I was drowning. It was dark blue but it turned brown in the water, which was very unfortunate. It would look like a brown kilt that had been in a hurricane. There was an Italian boy in my class at school called Nino Manibli, who was very stylish. He had the best swimming costume you ever saw, all red-and-white satin with laces up both sides, and there was I, in blue-turning-brown-wool with a belt. I used to fantasise about murdering Nino in his bed to steal his costume.

Florence and I would swim at Rothesay beach and beneath the water my costume would transform into a drogue parachute. The crotch would be down around my knees, as if I was being pursued by a dark blue nappy. It would slow me down: I would swim my hardest and go nowhere. When I came out of the water, I had to grab the back of my costume and pull it back in order to pull the front up and stop my family jewels flopping out and scaring the other children on the beach. The costume would be running like a tap and it would look as if I was peeing myself on the sand. After I'd been swimming, it would take two weeks to dry out.

I wasn't the only guy with a knitted costume, though. They were a big thing. Sometimes we would swim in the swimming pool in Rothesay. It had a café underneath it with windows into the pool and you could see the people's legs. So, there would be headless people swimming, flailing around, trying to keep their costume on, with the crotch flapping around their ankles, while people were trying to eat their scones:

> *'Mummy, Mummy, what's that?'*
> *'Look away! Look away, Lucinda! Cover your eyes! I think that*
> *man is having a fit! And that might be a haemorrhoid!'*

One of Rothesay's major tourist attractions was its Victorian toilets. They made an extraordinary fuss about those. Tourists from all over the world would faithfully troop into the toilet to gaze reverentially upon the cisterns. Or, at least, the male tourists would – they were men's toilets so women weren't allowed in.

Our two weeks in Rothesay would be over in no time and we'd be back at the harbour waiting for the ferry home. The incoming Paisley holidaymakers would all come down the gangway and my father would tell Florence and me, 'Go and give your buckets and spades away.' We'd go up to children coming off the boat and give them to them, and off they'd go on holiday with our buckets and spades.

Rothesay was a curious place but when I was a wee boy it felt like Paradise. Those two weeks were the highlight of my year. I've been back many times as an adult, of course, and learned about its history. The town was first built by a Viking called Magnus Bareleg, who was a bit of a fucking hooligan. Everybody was scared of him and they only got rid of him by giving him the Isle of Orkney as a birthday present. Old Bareleg was delighted and moved there right away. The town has also got a beautiful old Art Deco theatre, the Rothesay Pavilion, which I have played a few times and which is being restored at the moment. But my strongest memories of Rothesay are all from my childhood holidays – like the time that a fucking jackdaw landed on my head and nearly gave me a coronary.

In the Fifties and Sixties, Scottish holidaymakers lived in hope of getting their holiday for free if they spotted the *Sunday Post*'s HON-man, or Holiday for Nothing-man. He was a furtive individual in a trench coat who supposedly hung around the nation's seaside resorts with a copy of the *Sunday Post* under his arm. If anybody spotted him and said, 'I know you're the HON-man and I claim my prize,' they got a ten-shilling note, or maybe a pound, which would basically pay for the whole holiday. Nobody I know ever glimpsed this elusive creature.

When I was a boy the *Sunday Post* used to sell close on two million copies a week, which wasnae bad for a country of five million people. People used to buy ten copies at once and send them off to aunts and uncles who had emigrated to America or Australia, in order to remind them what a fucking weird country Scotland was. The *Sunday Post* was a great source of unintentional comedy. It used to give out sage advice to its readers. I remember reading it once and it said: *'An ideal thing for these slippery days is to wear your thick socks outside of your shoes. They get good traction in the snow.'*

I always imagined some old guy taking heed of that pearl of wisdom before he went off to the shops to buy his groceries. He would be trudging along and somebody would say, 'You stupid old bugger! Get yourself home and put your shoes on!' They would take him home and fling him in his house. The poor old sod would starve to death because every time he tried to get to the shop, people would bring him back.

People bought the *Sunday Post* for fifty years and read their cartoon strips, *Oor Wullie* and *The Broons*, hoping against hope that one day they would be funny. They were always sorely disappointed. Or they would write in to the *Sunday Post* doctor: 'I have a lump appearing under my armpit. What should I do?' 'You should go to the fucking doctor!' A friend of mine used to carry around a clipping from the *Sunday Post* doctor because he loved it so much. It said: *'Never eat mince on a clammy day.'*

There must have been many disappointed conversations up and down the land:

> *'Mother, can we have mince today?'*
> *'No, son, it's a wee bit clammy.'*

As a kid I was bought up on chips, mince and tatties and bangers and mash. Scottish health food! It was great. If my family were on holiday, we might go to a chip shop and have a fish high tea – fish and chips with bread and butter – but I never went into a restaurant until I was in my twenties. I played a folk gig in Ayr and the promoter invited me for a Chinese meal afterwards. I was genuinely scared to go because I didn't know what to do, or what to order, or even what Chinese food was. But I remember being amazed at just how good it tasted and feeling delighted to discover a whole new world of food that I had never known about.

Food has always been a major bone of contention when people talk about Scotland. I think it's fair to say that we don't have the very best culinary reputation in the world. The Scottish sweet tooth is a legendary thing and critics allege there is a great desire in Scotland to deep-fry any food that is left hanging around. I've never actually seen a deep-fried Mars Bar or Bounty, although I did once see them advertised in a chip shop. However, I confess that I have had a deep-fried jam sandwich, and I can report back that it was delicious.

Porridge is really important in Scotland. When you are a wee boy you have sugar in your porridge and then at some point you grow into a man and have it with salt instead. Somebody – it is usually an uncle – will come around your house, and laugh at you: 'Oh, you're still having your porridge with sugar, are you? That's rubbish!' Then you start having it with salt, and you don't really like it but you say, 'Aye, that's great!' because it makes you feel like a man.

I am still a puritan with porridge. I have it boiled in water, not milk, then I add cold milk and salt to it. That sounds very Presbyterian and hard-line but it's how I like it. Hotel staff always look at me askance when I ask them to make it like that. My wife has it with brown sugar and raisins and honey and loads of stuff and it's lovely but it isnae porridge. I tell her: 'Christ almighty, Pamela! It looks like a dessert!'

People call eating porridge 'getting your oats' and the reason is that they saw the effect that eating oats has on horses. It makes them all jiggly-wiggly. I know that rural workers in Scotland used to pour their porridge into a drawer in the sideboard and leave it to harden, then cut it into squares and carry it off to work in their sporrans to eat while they were out in the fields. The weirdest thing that I ever did with my porridge was to let it go cold and hard, and then spread Vegemite on it and eat it cold.*

Another great Scottish delicacy is tablet, which is like a super-sweet fudge. If you're eating tablet you might as well just open a packet of sugar and pour it into your mouth because the effect on your teeth and your health will be exactly the same. I love it, though. I am in show business so I am supposed to take the high road when it comes to healthy eating, but . . . fuck it! I'm Scottish! My children make tablet and we all sit down and wolf into it together. My first father-in-law was a great tablet maker. He would make it on a tea tray then carve it up into squares in the traditional Scottish style.

As a Scotsman, I obviously know that fat improves any food. I can never get enough of lorne sausages – Scottish square sausages – which are meat and rusks cooked in bags and bags of fat. In fact, I wrote a wee poem about a sausage. It's called 'I'd Rather Be a Sausage':

---

* Whoopi Goldberg said to me that eating Vegemite is like licking a cat's arse. That made me wonder how she had done her research.

I'd rather be a sausage than a British man of war
Or a caterpillar with a broken arm.
Corduroy braces are all very well
And give no immediate cause for alarm.
But the sausage is a mighty beast who cares only to please
In fact, he is the mightiest there is.
Content to lie in frying pans for hours at a stretch
Singing sizzle, sizzle, sizzle, sizzle, siz.

I think it may be proof that you are mentally ill when you are writing things like that. Desserts for me should be like 1950s school-dinner puddings. My ultimate in dessert is sponge and custard, or vanilla ice cream with chocolate sauce. I can't be doing with toff food and middle-class crap like Îles Flottantes and Blue Lagoons with Meringues. I eat it, if I have to, but I've never shaken off my basic working-class palate, nor have I attempted to.

Scotland has always had a great attitude towards its sweet tooth and its sugar addiction. Scottish people will read a report that says that Scotland has the highest figures for stomach cancer in the world due to its bad diet, and they will say: *'Yes! We're Number One in the world! Number One! Don't you forget it!'* Yet even Scotland is becoming more health-conscious now. I come back to Glasgow and go to restaurants and I notice on the menus that there are 'healthy versions' of traditional Scottish dishes such as Cullen Skink. There are gyms dotted around everywhere and people are marching off to them and being terribly fit, but I don't think they are any the better for it. Quite frankly, I think if more chip shops opened up, *that* would be better for them.

Living in the US, there are certain Scottish delicacies that I miss. I miss very much a thing that we call a plain loaf. It's white bread with a black crust at one end and a white crust at the other and it is just delicious, especially toasted. I sometimes lie in bed in Florida and fantasise about a Scottish plain loaf.*

When I come back to Scotland I always hear words that I used to use as a boy and a young man but have kind of stopped through living away for so many years. It's great to hear them again and they make me smile. The Scottish language is a strange and wonderful thing. Scottish people have always enjoyed playing with it. We invent our own words, derived from Gaelic and Anglo-Saxon and all sorts of sources. When I watch Celtic, I still call a throw-in a '*shy*' and a goal-kick a '*bye*'. Those phrases are nearly dead now; not many people say them any more, but I cling on to them.

Some words fit really well in Scottish mouths. Instead of saying, 'I'm afraid,' people say, 'I'm feart,' or 'I had fear,' or 'I was feart.' Another word that I love is '*glaikit*'. It means gormless. You might say, 'You know a *glaikit* guy will button his jacket wrong,

---

* It's safe to say that grocery shopping in America is a very, very different business from in Glasgow. I remember the first time I went to a supermarket in Los Angeles I was staring at a wall of different kinds of milk, completely dumbfounded. There was a sign next to them that said, 'Guaranteed to contain no dairy products'.

have one button up and one down.' 'Aye, he looked full *glaikit* with his jacket like that.' And you don't find many older people in Scotland saying 'baby' – it's always a *'wean'*.

That's how we all talked at home and when we were playing out in the street when we were growing up. We talked Scots because that is what we are. It's our language and it should be used and admired and developed but that doesnae happen. Kids get told at school by some prick of an English teacher that they are speaking slang, but they're not – they're talking Scots. All of their lives, Scottish people have been accused of using slang and had their culture messed about with. It's wrong and it hurts Scots to hear that – especially when it comes from their own people. There are some interfering fucking *glaikit* people out there.

Scotland is a great country and I've not remotely got any kind of victim syndrome but I do occasionally think that Scots get a wee bit of a raw deal in the way we are viewed. I've heard it said before that Scots keep arguments and feuds going for a lot longer than people from other countries. I don't think that's right at all – I think they're *just talking*. Scottish people enjoy talking. I saw some report by an American university that Scottish folk are genetically programmed to keep disputes going! I think that is a load of shit. That is the kind of conclusion that people come to when they have nothing better to do with their time.

I like to know where and what I've come from so I have read a lot of Scottish history over the years, and one thing I've learned is the importance of bagpipes in Scottish culture and folklore. I have always loved bagpipes and what they call the *pibroch*, which is the classical music of the pipes. I like them in the same way that I like Indian music, and for the same reason – that gorgeous droning classicism.

When I used to go to the Highland Games there would be marching bands and bands playing for dancers, but there would also be a pibroch competition. This is where one piper at a time plays while marching incredibly slowly – walking like a newt – being marked and judged as he goes. I used to lie down in the grass and shut my eyes and listen to the pibroch players. They are just utterly magnificent.*

People who don't share my affection for the bagpipes may feel they are just an infernal racket or else some kind of noisy confidence trick to drum up the tourist trade, but there is a whole lot more to them than that. Scotland has always had a high regard for bagpipers because they used to lead us into battle. There's a famous story from the First World War of a piper in France leading four Scottish fighters across a no-man's land between the trenches. As they marched towards the enemy, the piper was playing a grand, swirling attack tune:

---

* For many years, Pamela and I had a place in Aberdeenshire, and every year a local pipe band would march up my drive, play some music, then do the same at the homes of the other local lairds. This was a tradition that had been going on there for centuries and I loved being part of it and keeping it going.

'Dee-dee diddle-de-diddle-de-diddle-dee!'

The four fighters and the piper were striding on but then a burst of machine-gun fire came from inside a German trench:

'Ack-ack-ack-ack-ack-ack!'

One of the soldiers fell, mortally wounded, so now it was just three fighters and the piper. They carried on marching:

'Dee-dee diddle-de-diddle-de-diddle-dee!'

More artillery fire came from the Germans:

'Ack-ack-ack-ack-ack-ack!'

Another brave fighter fell dead so now there were just two soldiers left, marching behind the piper:

'Dee-dee diddle-de-diddle-de-diddle-dee!'
'Ack-ack-ack-ack-ack-ack!'

Another soldier dropped dead, leaving just one Scottish fighter and the piper. At which point, that soldier turned to the piper and said:

'Can you no play something that they fucking like?'

But in all seriousness, bagpipes actually have played a major role in Scottish history. In 1645 there was a bloody siege at Duntrune Castle in Argyll, the home of the Campbell clan, who had a nasty reputation as being bastards and were entirely deserving of it. Their bitter rivals, the MacDonalds, got wind that there weren't many Campbells in place in the castle at the time so they decided to come down and drive them out. They laid siege to the castle, killed a few Campbells and took the place over. Then they celebrated in the traditional Scots way with parties, whisky and bagpipes.

The Campbells – who were away – heard about what had happened and were less than delighted. They showed up en masse at Duntrune and slaughtered the MacDonalds. They killed everybody in the castle except for the bagpiper, whom they kept as a souvenir and for entertainment. This poor guy would look out from the castle over the loch, waiting for the MacDonalds to come back and save him. One day he saw an attack boat full of MacDonalds sailing over the loch towards the castle: 'Ah, great, here's my guys!' But the piper knew that the Campbells had also seen the invaders coming, were lying in wait for them in vast numbers in the castle and would massacre them. So, he started playing a stirring tune to welcome the MacDonalds but he purposely put two bum notes in:

'Dee-dee diddle-de-diddle-doh-thump-doh-diddle-dee!'

The approaching MacDonald chieftain heard the tune and the duff notes and correctly recognised that the piper was giving them a warning. He turned his army around and headed for safety. The Campbells realised what the piper had done and, understandably, were not best pleased. They cut off his hands so he could never do it again and he bled to death: a horrible and gruesome way to go. People say that after his murder the piper haunted the castle and would pipe across the loch in the gloaming.

Duntrune Castle changed hands again in the eighteenth century and many years later, in 1880, they were doing some work on it and somebody lifted up a flagstone. Underneath was a skeleton . . . with no hands. It was the piper, and they had him buried in an Episcopalian ceremony. But, of course, the piper was a Catholic and so was less than happy about this. Word is that he still haunts the place, playing his bum notes:

'Dee-dee diddle-de-diddle-doh-thump-doh-diddle-dee!'

Although I have always loved the important signifiers of Scottish life and culture, such as the rolling mountains, the wild, beautiful lochs of the Highlands and islands, and the bagpipes, I couldn't stand a lot of the Scottish popular entertainers who made their names and forged careers on the back of them. I call them the Scottish shortbread people, because they are like singing shortbread tins. There is so much great real folk music in Scotland but these guys have totally bypassed it in order to sing chintzy wee tra-la-la songs written by people in London who have probably never been to Scotland in their lives. One of those songwriters got found out many years ago. He wrote a song called 'The Blue Misty Hills of Tiree'. If you're ever been to Tiree, it's as flat as a billiard table.

I don't begin to understand what these singers, these *tartan people*, think they are doing. When I was young, the television would always push these guys, who always had a gap in their teeth and their wee badger handbag, warbling away: *'Och aye, the mountains and the rivers, diddle-diddle-diddle-aye!'* Even as a boy, I knew they were shit. I would look at them and think, *What are you doing?* But a lot of Scottish people don't share my disdain for all of that cheesy crap. Scotland is a place where many of the locals collect the tourist shit and display it as ornaments in their own homes. You go in their houses and you find Loch Ness Monsters and wee kilt-y men proudly arrayed across the mantelpiece.

I always thought the worst of the Scottish shortbread men was Harry Lauder. He was a vaudeville and music hall singer and comedian and it was impossible to escape him in the Forties and Fifties. Believe it or not, he was the first British performer to sell a million records. He would trill these cutesy faux-Scottish ditties like 'Roamin' in the Gloamin'' and 'A Wee Deoch-an-Doris' and 'A Wee Hoose 'mang the Heather' and 'I Love a Lassie' and he had this awful false little laugh: *'Ha ha ha, ho ho ho!'* I was allergic to the fucker. When I did my *Big Wee Tour of Britain*, back in the Seventies, I opened it with my huge hairy head sticking through a life-size cut-out of Lauder as I sang one of his songs: 'Keep Right on to the End of the Road'. Then I said, 'Friends, Romans, Countrymen: I come to bury Lauder, not to praise him!' The cut-out was whisked away and there I stood, in a polka-dot suit, a Scottish comedian with nothing to do with Harry Lauder and his old ways of doing things.

Andy Stewart was another of the tartan people, the guy who used to host the Hogmanay shows on TV every New Year's Eve. He wasn't as bad as Lauder – not many people were – and the one time that I met him he was extremely nice to me. But I think when I first appeared, I did a lot of harm to those singing shortbread tins. I knackered their business. They had all been touring Australia and America and Canada for years with their cosy, tourist-friendly version of Scotland. But then I started to tour a very different, more modern version of Scotland, and it kind of blew them away. Blew them right away into the mountains and the gloaming.

The good thing is that the tartan people can't do their tired old shtick any more because Scotland is changing. *Scotland has changed.* It is well connected up to the rest of the world nowadays and most people don't want to hear someone singing, 'Och aye, the mountains and the rivers!' or listen to 'A Wee Hoose 'mang the Heather' today. When I travelled around the country during summer 2018, Scotland showed me many surprises, but for me none was bigger or better than meeting the Syrian refugees on the Isle of Bute.

I met a 21-year-old guy there called Malek Helmi. He and his family had to flee Syria in February 2016. His father, Bashar, used to have a factory in Damascus that made baby clothes but it got burned down. Malek's family had all relocated to Rothesay under a refugee scheme: his immediate family then uncles, aunties, grandfathers, grandmothers, the whole works. Malek introduced me to his 'wee-est' brother, who had a wonderful broad Argyll accent, and he told me that, after a difficult start, the family had settled in Rothesay, been accepted on Bute and made great friends with the locals. Malek was about to head off to a Scottish university to study molecular biology.

The Helmi family had even started their own business in Rothesay, baking bread and selling it on the pier to people getting off the ferry and at the island's Sunday market. In summer 2018, Bashar opened his own bakery, Helmi's Patisserie, in the town and it is already doing a roaring trade. They sold out of everything in the shop on the very first day and they are continuing to do so. As Malek told me, with his twinkling eyes and in his new broad Scots brogue, about all his hopes and plans, and all the great friends he had made on Rothesay, I felt so proud, as a Scotsman, that the people on the island had made these Syrian refugees so welcome. Here they were, making a new home in the funny place where I had swum in my knitted costume and got clonked round the ear for not being able to tell the time sixty-five years ago, and they were making an amazing job of it. I found it mind-boggling that they had accomplished so much in such a short time in a foreign country: in Scotland.

I have done many things in my life but I try to imagine myself, at the same young age as Malek, uprooting and moving halfway across the world to Syria, settling in and setting up a Scottish bakery, and I can't begin to imagine how I would ever have done it. It's a credit to him and to his family, and it's a credit to the people of Bute for accepting the refugees so well. It shows me how much Scotland has changed in my lifetime, and it makes my old heart very proud and happy.

'THE DEPARTURE LOUNGE IS GETTING VERY CROWDED'

The world turns and life moves on. I have lived in America for a long time now and I reminisce a lot about Glasgow but when I return, I realise that I am a tourist in my own hometown. I don't have a house there any more, and every time I come back, more and more things have changed. Restaurants have moved and they have put a ring road in and I don't know the way to certain places. I have to work it all out again.

There's a river bridge that was built in 2006 but it still feels new to me. It's called the Clyde Arc but no one in Glasgow has ever called it the Clyde Arc. In fact, I would take a wager that nobody in Glasgow even *knows* it is called the Clyde Arc. It's at an angle to the river, so from the moment that it was opened it's been known as the Squinty Bridge. Nobody knows who called it the Squinty Bridge. The whole town came to the conclusion at the same time. In the same way they opened a big concert venue on the Clyde nearly twenty years ago, next to the SECC. They tried to call it the Clyde Auditorium but no one in Glasgow knew it as that. They called it the Armadillo, because that is what it looks like – a huge concrete-and-steel armadillo. The owners eventually gave up and changed its name to the SEC Armadillo. My grandson has gone one better – he calls it the Croissant, which he says it resembles more. I think he is right.

I do notice one major difference when I come back to Glasgow now, though. The very feel of the place, *the air*, has changed. As I used to say on stage, Glasgow used to be a black city, as if it had been drawn in ink. Now it has lost its industry it looks like a water-colour, as if someone has learned to work the skylight and let the light in. When I was a boy, Glasgow was all docks and shipyards and steelworks and foundries, employing thousands and thousands of people. Now it has become a service-industry city of offices and cafés and pubs and restaurants.

I always love coming back to Glasgow. I remember talking to a good friend of mine, the actor Jimmy Copeland: he's another one who is dead now. He was a Glaswegian who lived in London, and he said that every time he came back, he loved getting off the train at Central Station because he could feel Glasgow *coming up through the soles of his feet*. He told me a great story about that. He said one time he got off the train, excited to be in Glasgow, and there was a guy walking down the platform towards him. The guy put his hand up as if to greet him, so Jimmy put his own hand up back, but instead the guy put his hand to his nostril and blew snot on to the platform.

• • • • • • • •

People in Glasgow, and in Scotland, have a healthy regard and a healthy disregard for each other. They tend not to hide their feelings. They are very open and direct about whether they like or dislike each other and I find that very healthy and refreshing. I still have the same friends I have always had: most of my surviving best pals are in Scotland. People are often astonished just how few show business friends I have. If it wasn't for Eric Idle, I think I wouldn't have any.

My grandkids in Glasgow are growing up in a very different society, and a much better society, than I did seventy years ago. They are very well balanced. Wally, my grandson, doesn't have any clichéd, bigoted views on Catholics or Protestants, or what French or Italian people are like. He takes life as it comes. His favourite football player is Lionel Messi and his British team is Arsenal – as a Glaswegian! I love that, and I love seeing little kids walking around the city with Real Madrid or Barcelona jerseys on. They seem to have much broader minds in their appreciation of everything and the world around them. Like me, they are citizens of the world who happen to be Scottish.*

---

* Loving Scotland is not the same as being a patriot. I'm not a patriot. One thing that I have never had any interest in is hating England and the English. I like Thomas Hardy as much as I like Robert Burns. I'm an Anglophile and I have been ever since my father first took me to England as a wee boy. As an Anglophile, I've never shouted for Scottish independence – but I might be changing my mind now.

When I was back in Scotland a lot in summer 2018 I found that my fame and my popularity were a lot more than I thought they would be. People seem to have got a bit frantic about me because of my Parkinson's. I think my knighthood has made me more popular than I used to be, as well. The attention on me when I go walking around has increased to an extraordinary degree and I've never known anything like it. There seems to be a lot more fuss being made of me, by men, women *and* children. When I come back, everybody makes me very welcome.

People have always approached me in the street but now it happens so much that it's hard for me to get anywhere I want to go when I'm in Scotland. I have had it for many years and it is very pleasant. You never quite get used to it but it has become part of my life that I accept and mostly enjoy. I have known people who run away from their fame and the attention. They go into hiding and I have never understood that. It must cause them more angst than it deserves. I've always found it ludicrous to be scared of the people who made you.

The Brexit vote is a disaster and the breaking up of the togetherness of Europe is a crime bordering on a sin. Europe did something unique and important when it created the European Community. It meant European nations couldn't fight each other and it has stopped war since the 1940s, which is extraordinary. I think the more people are together, not separate, the happier they will be. The most important thing for Scotland is to keep our contact with Europe. Scots voted to stay in Europe and if the only way for us to do that is to become independent from England, that may just be the way to go. And I never thought I would say that.

Lately the uproar has been extraordinary, though.* I was walking across a car park in Glasgow recently. I passed a hairdressers' shop and it emptied out. The women all ran out with their wet hair to get a selfie with me. That evening I went out with my daughter and my grandchildren for Chinese food and the manager of the restaurant came over and said, 'There's a girl at a table over there who'd like a picture with you.' We took it, and then lots of other people came up to take photos of me holding their babies and all sorts. When we left at the end of the night, the whole restaurant applauded. Even after all these years, it feels weird. But it means a lot to me.

Everybody wants a selfie these days. The autograph seems to be a thing of the past. Sometimes people get tongue-tied. They run up and say 'Hello!' then they stop talking and they're not sure what to do next. I'm not sure what to do either, so we both stand there with our arms hanging by our sides, until we call it to an ungainly end. I remember once, after I'd played a gig at the Armadillo, I was outside the venue doing selfies with fans on their mobiles. One guy came up with a proper camera and asked if he could take a photo. I looked at it and said: 'What kind of camera is that? You can't even

---

* For one thing there are big mural portraits of me up on walls all over Glasgow, to celebrate my seventy-fifth birthday. That left me absolutely flabbergasted. They are these big fifty-foot paintings by Rachel Maclean, Jack Vettriano and my old mate, John Byrne, and when I saw them they completely stunned me. It had such a profound effect on me, that these genius people should have taken the time and gone to so much trouble for me. Before I saw them, I thought that I would be laughing and joking about them but they took my breath away.

make a phone call on it!' The poor guy was so nervous that he started to apologise: 'I'm so sorry, I left my phone at home!' I had to assure him that I was only kidding.

Rock stars get mobbed when they go out but that is just by young people. My demographic seems to go from pre-school to old-age pensioners. I understand that, though. I'm seventy-five and I have been doing what I do since I was in my twenties, so people have known me for fifty years. Anyone in their fifties or younger has known me their entire life. If they have liked what I do, or admired it, for fifty years, it must be quite a shock to suddenly be confronted by me, and I take that into consideration.

Some people greet me like we're actually family. It's like I'm a long-lost cousin. They get a selfie, then other people notice us and want theirs, and the crowd around me just grows and grows. It gets bigger and bigger and I'm stuck on the corner of a street taking selfies for person after person, and a sort of panic comes over me: *How am I going to get out of this situation? Am I here for the rest of my life?* Then the attention can become a bit of a pain – but normally, it's great. It would be highly churlish to complain about it.

I'm very lucky, actually – in Scotland, I can get away with murder. If I am walking down the street and there are men down a hole digging or fixing some sewage pipes or some such, I like to stop and say to them, *'Come on, put your backs into it! No wonder this country is in the state it's in!'* I'm lucky because they will burst out laughing. If anybody else said it to them, they would get a kick in the arse. They would be up out of the hole and after them.

I guess I just feel lucky to have had such a long career and to be loved and admired after all that time. Generally, my life is a joy. People come up every day and tell me how nice it is to see me – what the fuck is wrong with that? It just means that I have a funny idea of what the world is like. I think that everybody is always laughing and smiling because, to me, they are.

Being seventy-five takes some getting used to you. *Being old* takes some getting used to. When I turned sixty, I thought, *pfft, so what?* and I had a great big party. But turning seventy felt different. People start to phone you up *just to see if you are OK*. They say, 'I assume you won't be having a party – you'll be having a nice wee rest.'

I think the whole thing of acting your age is deeply over-rated. Acting your age is about as sensible as acting your street number. There's no sense to it. But I have to admit that odd things happen to you that you have to pay attention to. You start to make involuntary noises. Hair sprouts where it didn't grow before. I used to trim my nose hair once every twenty-seven years and now it is twice every three weeks. I had my beard in a little diamond for ages but I started to drool so I have broadened out my beard to soak up the drool. Because *nobody wants drooling banjos*.

Then the people you have known all of your life start dying. Not so long ago I was talking to a very dear friend, the Irish musician Phil Coulter, in Dublin. We were talking about all of the Irish folk singers and pipers and musicians that we have known and played with over the years and how many of them had died in the previous few months. I thought aloud: 'A lot of them have passed, recently, haven't they?'

'Yes,' said Phil. 'The departure lounge is getting very crowded.'

He's right. I die in every movie that I'm in nowadays. My children are sick of it.*

Of course, my Parkinson's disease dominates my life to quite a large degree nowadays. It occupies a lot of my thinking time every single day. When I go into a restaurant, I have to look around and work out where to sit and choose somewhere that it won't take me a long time to get up from. I sometimes ask the waiter, 'Listen, I might have trouble getting out of this chair when I have finished eating – will you hang about and help me?' They always say yes. People in general are very nice to me and keep telling me that I'm looking good. I think they are relieved that I'm not all shaky.

The thing that I find hardest about my Parkinson's is coming to grips with the fact that *it's never going to go away*. Everything that has ever been wrong with me in the past always went away, eventually.

---

* I remember being in Australia in 2011 when Gerry Rafferty's daughter, Martha, phoned me up. She was with Gerry and said that he was in a bad way and on his deathbed, and would I like to talk to him? I said, 'Yes, of course,' but Martha said that Gerry was not in a frame of mind to be talking on the phone – would I be able to text him? So, I started texting him and trying to make him laugh and remind him of the old days, like the time that we smoked the Bible. Martha said later that Gerry was rolling with laughter, and that she hadn't known we had done half of the things that I was texting him about. The funniest thing was, not so long after, I was walking along in London and I bumped into Martha . . . and we were on Baker Street.

It was either operated on or it cured itself. This isn't going anywhere: in fact, it's going to get worse. My medication controls it for now, but in the very early days after I was first diagnosed they took me off it because the doctors reckoned the side effects were stronger than the positive effects. I asked them, 'What *are* the side effects?' They told me: 'An overriding interest in sex and gambling.' So, if you see somebody in Las Vegas with an erection, he has probably got Parkinson's.

I have talked to other people who have it. The actor Ian Holm, who I was in the *Hobbit* film with, advised me that when my hand starts to shake too much, I should put it into my pocket. 'That's OK,' I said to him, 'but what if I put it into my trouser pocket and I happen to be in an art gallery at the time, innocently examining the female nudes?' Robin Williams and I used to talk about Parkinson's a lot. He would call me up and we would compare notes and symptoms. Robin worried about it a lot. He got quite luvvie towards the end, and the last time that he phoned me, before he died, he told me that he loved me. I said that I loved him, too, and he said, *'No, I love you like a brother – do you realise that?'* I told him that I did, because I did.

I've only been on tour once since I got diagnosed with Parkinson's. I wasn't sure how it was going to go because I knew that my body was different, so I thought the best thing to do was to acknowledge it. I came on stage to 'Whole Lotta Shakin' Goin' On', and when the audience applauded me, I said, 'Och, you're only doing that because I'm not well!' I explained to them at the start that I have

Parkinson's disease and that they shouldn't worry about my left arm, which might creep up until I looked as if I was carrying an invisible raincoat. When my hand started to shake during the show, I showed them: 'Look, look!' I *just got on with it*. As simple as that.

The Parkinson's has trapped me a little in my shows now in that I can't prowl the stage any more like I used to. If I went to move, I limped, and I didn't want to do that, so I just stayed where I was, mostly rooted to the spot, and moved my hands at waist level. I described things with my hands the way I used to do when I was younger and used a mic stand. It was all very organic and very pleasant and the audience didn't seem to mind. I was getting the laughs every bit as much as before – maybe even better than before.

I have come off the road now and I haven't been playing any shows because of the Parkinson's, but I would like to do more. I don't know what the future holds in that respect because I don't know what state I will be in. Researchers are making progress on curing the disease but it all seems to be well away in the distance. I've spoken to guys working on it at Harvard and told them I'll be a guinea pig for them. I think they are going to take me up on that.

Having Parkinson's disease – and being seventy-five – has inevitably made me think sometimes about my death, but those thoughts go away as quickly as they come. I tend not to dwell on them. Somebody asked me if I wanted to join a suicide society. It's some organisation in Edinburgh that helps people to commit suicide and I believe that a lot of Parkinson's sufferers choose that course of action. But I don't want to. I'm too interested in what is going on around me. In any case, the fuckers didn't even offer me a lifetime membership.

I think life and death is a very simple question that is made far too complex by people who have an axe to grind. I think that when you die, you go to where you were before you were born: *nowhere*. But I see myself ending up my days in Scotland. I definitely fancy a grand parade through Glasgow, carrying my flower-strewn coffin to a magnificent marquee in George Square. I would like there to be a lot of gnashing of teeth and weeping children:

'Billy Connolly's away now!'

I have thought of being cremated and scattered on Loch Lomond, with a horizontal mourning stone so that tourists and locals can have a nice cup of tea on it. But I think I want to become part of Scotland when I die. In a coffin, you just turn to dust, so I would prefer to be buried in a wicker casket or in a sheet, like the Africans do, so that I actually become part of the earth. I would like a tree to be planted on top of me. And I told Pamela a long time ago the epitaph that I want on my gravestone:

JESUS CHRIST, IS THAT THE TIME ALREADY?*

---

* Failing that, I would like an epitaph in writing so tiny that visitors would have to inch right next to my gravestone to read it. It would say:
YOU'RE STANDING ON MY BALLS.

INDEX

Page references in *italics* indicate images.

BC indicates Billy Connolly.

INDEX

. . . .

INDEX

• • • • • • • •

INDEX

· · · · · · · ·

INDEX

INDEX

• • • • • • • • •

CREDITS

Picture Credits

Picture research completed by Victoria Hall.

All images © Mike Reilly, except for the following: Alamy p151, picture section 1 p2 bottom, p4 middle right, p5 middle, p6 top, p7 middle left, p7 bottom, p8 middle left; BBC p149; Billy Connolly picture section 1 p2 top, p4 top, p8, picture section 2 p1 bottom, p2 middle, p6 top; Getty Images p9, p50, p52, p53, p105, p140, p146, picture section 1 p1 middle, p2 middle, p3 bottom right, p4 middle left, p5 top, p5 bottom, p7 top, p7 bottom left, p8 bottom, picture section 2 p1 top, p2 top right, p3 top and bottom, p4 middle, p6 middle right, p7 middle right, p8 middle right and bottom; Gerald Blaikie/www.scotcities.com p187; Glasgow City Council picture section 2 p5 top; Mirrorpix picturex section 2 p2 top left, p5 middle; PA Images p1, picture section 1 p1 top, p3 top, p3 bottom left, picture section 2 p4 top, p6 bottom, p7 top; Reuters picture section 1 p6 middle; Thomas Nugent p43.

Text credits

'The Song of the Clyde' composed and written by R.Y. Bell and Ian Gourley; 'Ma! He's Making Eyes at Me' composed by Con Conrad, lyrics by Sidney Clare; 'Swanee' by Al Jolson, composed by George Gershwin, lyrics by Irving Caesar, published by Columbia records; 'What reader are you?' was created by booklikes.com; 'Heartbreak Hotel' by Elvis Presley, composed by Mae Boren Axton, lyrics by Tommy Durden, published by EMI; 'Donna' by Ritchie Valens, published my Warner Music; 'Dear Mary' by Slim Whitman, published by London Records; 'Any Dream Will Do' written by Andrew Lloyd Webber and Tim Rice; 'That's Amore' by Dean Martin, composer Harry Warren, lyrics by Jack Brooks, published by Capitol Records; 'Back to Dunoon' by Billy Connolly, *The Elephant's Graveyard* written by Peter McDougall, published by the BBC.

While every effort has been made to trace the owners of copyright material reproduced herein, the publishers would like to apologise for any omissions and will be pleased to incorporate missing acknowledgements in any future edition of this book.